MILITARY LEADERS
IN THE AMERICAN REVOLUTION

Dedicated to
The American Continental Army
—predecessor of the United States Army,
the first regular service of our Country—
who secured for us the blessings of liberty

2

MILITARY LEADERS IN THE AMERICAN REVOLUTION

By JOSEPH B. MITCHELL

EPM
PUBLICATIONS, INC.

McLean, Virginia

Books by Joseph B. Mitchell

MILITARY LEADERS IN THE CIVIL WAR
DECISIVE BATTLES OF THE CIVIL WAR
DECISIVE BATTLES OF THE AMERICAN REVOLUTION
TWENTY DECISIVE BATTLES OF THE WORLD (based upon Creasy)

Library of Congress Cataloging-in-Publication Data

Mitchell, Joseph B. (Joseph Brady), 1915–
   Military leaders in the American Revolution.

   Reprint. Originally published: New York: Putnam,
1967.
   Bibliography: p.
   Includes index.
   1. United States.   Continental Army—History.
2. United States—History—Revolution, 1775–1783.
3. United States—History—Revolution, 1775–1783—
Campaigns.   I. Title.
E259.M58 1989   973.3'4   89-1225
ISBN 0-939009-20-X

EPM Publications, Inc., 1003 Turkey Run Road,
McLean, VA 22101
Printed in the United States of America

Cover design by Tom Huestis

Foreword

This book was originally planned to be a study of military leaders of the American Revolution, British as well as American, possibly a German officer or two, including one or more of our French allies, with each individual presented in turn, chapter by chapter. With this concept, the first problem was to decide which of the many personalities to choose.

A list of possible choices was compiled. It included several American and British officers, as well as Lafayette, Rochambeau, and von Knyphausen. Then as time passed, the list grew longer and it became increasingly difficult to decide whom to select and whom to discard. Success in battle could not be a determining factor, for in the long run, none of the British or German leaders had been successful in the normally accepted meaning of the word. Yet some of these enemy commanders had shown great leadership ability and had come close to surmounting the problems facing them. Perhaps a useful criterion for selection could be—how well had each done with the means at hand?

The list of possibilities was again reviewed, paying particular attention to the way in which each commander attempted to solve the problems that confronted him at a crucial point in his career. Now my attention became focused upon the material available to each leader, in other words, the soldiers upon whom the commander in question had to rely. Almost all books and other writings on the Revolution have been based on the popular notion that the war was won by an untrained, patriotic people led by amateur generals who, in some miraculous manner, managed to create an army that defeated the trained soldiers of Europe. How could it be that we won this war without trained soldiers when a trained army has been essential in every other war in our history? Yet for nearly two hundred years, we have been repeatedly told that, in the American Revolution, the colonies rose in revolt, the minutemen sprang to arms, and the war was won. There is, of course, a certain element of truth in this American legend, but it has been tremendously exaggerated.

When my book *Decisive Battles of the American Revolution* was published, I was asked to give a speech about it to the American Revolution Round Table at Fraunces Tavern in New York City. On that occasion I expressed the opinion that the real heroes of the war were not the men who turned out to fight for their homes and firesides, to defend their farms and towns when the enemy came near. Although these individuals are most often praised by our historians and patriotic speakers, they actually contributed far less to the winning of the Revolution than the veterans of the Continental Army who left their houses and farms—not for a few days or weeks, but for years. They marched wherever they were told to go, hundreds of miles away from home; they were the dependable, trained nucleus around which the militia formed, the steadying influence in every major battle in which they participated.

At the end of my speech, the Chairman of the Round Table,

Professor North Callahan, suggested that I write a book about the Continental Army. His suggestion and the generous award by the Round Table of a bronze plaque for "the best book in this field for 1962" certainly influenced my decision to undertake another book on this subject, for in actual fact the greatest problem facing Washington and his generals throughout the Revolution was the building and maintaining of a regular army capable of facing its enemies on a battlefield.

The principal antagonist was, of course, the British Army, which had a worldwide reputation earned on countless battlefields. During the Revolution it may have been good wartime propaganda to poke fun at this army, but to continue this popular pastime for so many years after the war indicates a failure to appreciate the facts of the case. The British Army was a very worthy opponent indeed and performed remarkably well. To fail to give proper credit to it certainly does less than justice to those who eventually managed to defeat that army.

In time the American Revolution became a contest between the Continental Army, which was always understrength, and the British Army, which, because of its other worldwide commitments, had to be strengthened in America by German soldiers. To help fight against the Continentals, the British also created Loyalist units who fought side by side with British and German regulars. In addition, both the Americans and the British were forced to rely heavily on large numbers of untrained personnel. The most successful leaders on both sides were those who learned how to make the best use of their conglomerate forces.

At this point it became abundantly clear that the preconceived method of presenting each individual, chapter by chapter, could not be a satisfactory way of depicting the problems faced by either army. The book was started again, using the chronological approach, beginning with a description of General George Washington's struggle to build a Continental Army. From that point onward the choice of which military leaders to present became somewhat easier. Studies of Burgoyne and

Howe could describe why the British did not defeat the colonists in the early years. Then, in turn, other leaders could be introduced to illustrate progress in military thought, or lack of it. There was the risk that the book, because of the chronological order, might come to be thought of as a history rather than as a study of military leaders. However, it seemed safe enough to take this chance because a cursory glance at any history of the war would show immediately how many events described therein are barely mentioned here.

The selection of Washington, Burgoyne, and Howe established the pattern. Benedict Arnold's contributions to American success could not be overlooked. General Howe's successor, Sir Henry Clinton, was certainly worthy of study. Just as "Gentleman Johnny" Burgoyne had been the horrible British example of surprising incompetence, his American counterpart in almost all respects was Horatio Gates, whose failure at Camden must be studied to be appreciated in all its horror. By contrast, the contributions of Anthony Wayne and Daniel Morgan were refreshing. Though amateurs at the beginning, they developed into thoroughly capable, fully competent, efficient professional soldiers. Then, finally, for the purposes of this book, the climax is not Yorktown, but the great struggle for the south between Cornwallis, the best British general of the war, and Nathanael Greene, who was certainly second to no American commander except Washington.

The author feels that no apology is needed for not having dwelt at greater length upon the exploits of the Continental Navy. In a book of military leaders, naval heroes would be automatically excluded, although the important part played by sea power during the war was never overlooked. Nor does it seem necessary to mention that this book is not an effort to laud the Regular Army at the expense of the Reserves or the National Guard, for at the time of the Revolution there were no Reserves or National Guard as we know them today.

National Guard, for at the time of the Revolution there were no Reserves or National Guard as we know them today.

I would like to take this opportunity to express my appreciation to Charles Dwoskin for his helpful criticism, sound editorial advice, and for his patience with a book which took twice as long as either of us thought it would.

I again wish to express my gratitude to Janice Downey who made the maps for this book. On two previous occasions, for two other books, I have attempted to describe how much she has contributed. A military history without good maps is almost worthless. Here again, she has aided me immeasurably, improving my designs, rendering them more attractive, and executing them with skill, precision, and accuracy. I am greatly indebted to her.

Finally, I want to declare my heartfelt thanks to my wife Vivienne and to my family who cheerfully endured and encouraged the preparation of another of my books.

JOSEPH B. MITCHELL

Contents

MAPS

1

Washington and the Continental Army

Twenty-five miles apart from each other, two armies lay encamped. The commanding general and the majority of the troops of the larger and more powerful army had spent the greater part of the winter in comparative ease and security, peacefully enjoying many of the comforts of a large city, entirely surrounded by water, immune from attack.

The other army had shivered in small, inadequate, homemade huts, short of clothing and food, never knowing how many men would be present for duty, totally unable to defend itself, completely engrossed in a struggle to stay alive. It was now March, 1777, and that little army had fewer than 3,000 men fit for duty, of whom two-thirds were not regular soldiers and were due to return to their homes at the end of the month.

These two armies had been engaged in warfare against each other for nearly two years. On the surface, their conflict appeared extremely one-sided. On the one hand, the British Army enjoyed a worldwide reputation, earned on countless hard-fought battlefields. Its opponent, the Continental Army, representing the first thirteen states of the future United States of America, had almost been obliterated, but had managed, at the very last moment, to stage a comeback, and was now still in the process of formation.

When the American Revolution began on the village green at Lexington, there had been no Continental Army. The Americans who fought there and at Concord on April 19, 1775, were militia. Two months later, on June 17, the first big battle of the war was fought at Bunker Hill on the Charles-

13

town peninsula, one mile north of Boston. Again, no Continental troops were present because the Continental Congress had authorized the formation of an army only three days before, and the new commander-in-chief had not yet arrived on the scene.

The untrained American militia did so well in these battles that, unfortunately for the future of the country, the general public leaped to the wrong conclusion. It was proclaimed throughout the thirteen colonies that the trained British regular would be defeated by the freedom-loving colonial, fighting for a just cause, in defense of his home, and the principles he held sacred. People became convinced that patriotism was the sole qualification necessary to win this war.

Very few made any attempt to analyze what had really happened on these battlefields. In actual fact, nothing occurred that had not happened many times before in military history. The British retreat from Concord had demonstrated that untrained militia were capable of sniping at a retreating enemy on the march. Bunker Hill had proved that courageous, untrained men, if properly led, would hold their ground against a direct assault, when sheltered by fortifications. The New England farmers and townsmen who stood on the hill that day, and twice repulsed the British troops, were brave men and deserve all the praise that has been heaped upon them for generations. But they could not have done what the British soldiers facing them accomplished, nor is it any reflection upon their valor to admit this fact. Only courageous, trained troops could have returned again and again to attack the same place from which they had been thrown back twice with tremendous losses. Furthermore, there was no way in the world for the British soldier to know, when he was ordered to make his third assault, that the Americans had practically run out of ammunition.

From this battle the British leaders learned a lesson they never forgot. No matter how superior the training of the British Army might be, the American colonial was not to be despised when he was fighting for his life in a fortified position. Americans, on the other hand, made the completely false assumption that they had shown their superiority to the British regular. One cannot blame the average citizen of the American colonies too much for this mistaken notion, for there was no one in the colonies to tell him otherwise. Furthermore, even if there had been, there was no possible way for anyone to present the true facts to the general public. Nor would the people have been inclined to listen if there had been a way; distrust of a regular army had become too deeply ingrained into the public mind. Even after the war was over it was unpopular to talk about the trained American regular force, the Continental Army, without whom the war could not have been won. Orators and popular writers much preferred to talk at great length about what untrained militia had done. It was far more acceptable to do so than to proclaim the necessity for military service. Today, reputable historians are still writing that untrained troops led by amateur generals won the American Revolution.

Fortunately, however, the Continental Congress had taken action leading toward the establishment of a regular military organization. It had become increasingly apparent that the contest would eventually extend beyond the borders of New England. The support of the other colonies would be needed to prevent the dissolution of the force already gathered around Boston. Therefore, on June 14, the Congress had authorized the formation of a Continental Army. Ten companies of expert riflemen were to be raised: six in Pennsylvania, two in Maryland, and two in Virginia. This date is still observed as the birthday of the United States Army. Then on the following day, George Washington was chosen as commander-in-chief of "all continental forces, raised or to be raised, for the defense of American liberty."

When John Adams of Massachusetts nominated Washington, he was thinking of politics as much as of the new general's qualifications for the position. Washington was not a trained soldier. He had seen service in the French and Indian War, but so had a number of others who were given commissions in this new army. However, it was important to enlist southern sympathy for the cause, and no one could object to the choice because his reputation was widespread. He was well known throughout the colonies as a gentleman of character, a leader in whom the people could put absolute trust. His selection was to prove to be the wisest possible choice.

George Washington formally accepted the appointment on June 16, in a very modest speech. He thanked the members of the Congress, but declared, with the utmost sincerity, that he did not think himself fully qualified for the task. He also declined all payment for his services, asking only that he be reimbursed for his expenses.

There is no doubt that he lacked the military training and experience that the new appointment required, never having participated in operations on as large a scale as he would now be forced to supervise. Nevertheless he left to take command of the army surrounding Boston, resolved to do his duty to the best of his ability, no matter how trying it might prove to be. Enroute he was greeted by the news of Bunker Hill. When told that the militia had stood their ground, he is supposed to have exclaimed, "The liberties of the country are safe!"

Washington arrived, assumed command on July 3, 1775, and, in short order, became completely disenchanted with the militia. Most of the campsites were unsanitary, the command was disorganized, and discipline was almost completely lacking. In many instances the officers had been elected to their commands and, in order to retain their popularity, made no effort to control their men in any way. Sometimes, also, it was impossible to tell at a glance who the officers or noncommissioned officers were in an army without uniforms. Inquiries as to who was supposed to be the commander of a unit might produce the most astounding answers. One of Washington's staff discovered that, in one case at least, the company barber was apparently one of the officers.

To an aristocratic Virginia gentleman this was a tremendous shock. If he knew nothing else about forming an army, Washington was fully alive to the necessity of establishing a proper chain of command. He knew that an efficient corps of officers meant the difference between victory and defeat; an army without leadership and discipline is doomed.

It was manifestly impossible to supply uniforms to this mass of men; nor would it have been wise to do so. There were about 17,000 gathered there early in July, but the enlistments of all were due to expire by the end of the year. It was possible, however, to provide for some rank distinction by the fairly simple method of ordering the wearing of different colored ribbons, hat ornaments, and shoulder knots. Washington prescribed these in one of his earliest orders.

To aid him in his arduous task the Congress appointed four major generals: Artemas Ward of Massachusetts, who had previously been in charge of the men around Boston; Charles Lee, an experienced, professional, ex-British officer who could be expected to advise the commander-in-chief on military matters; Philip Schuyler of New York, whom Washington placed in command of the troops gathered in the northern part of that colony; and Israel Putnam of Connecticut, whose name was famous throughout New England for his exploits in the French and Indian War, and who was now one of the recent heroes of Bunker Hill.

Eight brigadier generals were also elected by the Congress: Seth Pomeroy, Richard Montgomery, David Wooster, William Heath, Joseph Spencer, John Thomas, John Sullivan, and Nathanael Greene. Then, in addition, Horatio Gates was appointed adjutant general, with the rank of brigadier. This proved to be a most fortunate choice for Gates was, like Charles Lee, a former British officer. Unlike Lee, however, he soon proved that he had a definite flair for administration. He became Washington's right-hand man in the extremely difficult job of organizing the army's administration. Of the other brigadiers, Washington had already noted that the camp of the Rhode Island brigade, commanded by Nathanael Greene, presented a neat, orderly appearance, in striking contrast to most of the other camps. These two officers were among the first the commander-in-chief singled out for special attention.

Confronted simultaneously with so many problems of discipline, training, organization, and administration, while at the same time faced with the task of maintaining the siege of Boston, it is difficult to say which weighed most heavily upon Washington's mind. Judging by his correspondence, though, the problem that worried him most was the formation of the Continental Army. His men were looking forward eagerly to returning home at the end of the year 1775. Somehow he had to persuade them to reenlist to serve through the year 1776. Large numbers were needed to maintain the siege and also to serve in the other departments, for example, in upper New York, where the colonists faced Canada.

The Continental Congress could not draft men into service. It had to rely entirely upon volunteers. The most important factor bearing on this problem was that the Congress had no authority to levy taxes or collect revenues. It was forced to issue bills of credit to be paid by the colonies at their convenience. These hazy promises to pay were not conducive to enlistment. The financial system thus rested almost entirely on the faith of the people that the American cause would ultimately triumph, and that sometime in the dim future these bills would be paid.

Furthermore, in 1775, almost everyone thought that the struggle would be of short duration. Even Washington was originally inclined toward that view. It has often been claimed that the Congress made a great mistake when it decided to limit the original enlistments to the year 1776, and that the enlistments should have been for three years or for the duration of the war. Yet, when we see how much trouble was encountered in enlisting men for only one year, we can guess that the number of men willing to serve three years would have been very small indeed. The colonial tradition established by the

18

French and Indian Wars was one of short-term service for a single campaign.

Foremost, however, in the mind of every man was the obvious fact that if he enlisted in the Continental Army, he could be forced to serve outside his own colony. Washington could try to persuade the men to join. He could set an example for them, but he could not stoop to curry favor with them as so many of the elected officers had done. Nor could he overcome the basic difference between service in the Continental Army and service in the militia. Continental service meant leaving their families to shift for themselves, by themselves, for long periods of time. The burden of trying to run their farms and manage their homes, to raise crops and market them, to look after their business would have to be borne entirely by their wives while they were gone, perhaps hundreds of miles away from their own colonies. Militia service was almost the complete reverse—short periods of being away, for only a few months at most, perhaps for only a few weeks. The wonder is not that the recruiting proceeded slowly, but that it proceeded at all. By mid-December, 1775, somewhat less than 6,000 men were enlisted, nowhere near the 20,000 that the Congress had envisioned. In order to maintain the siege, Washington was forced again to call upon the New England colonies to send militia to take the place of those who were leaving.

Fortunately, the militia came, and fortunately, also, the British in Boston remained inactive. While the Americans were replacing one army with another would have been a perfect time for the British to attack, but they failed to take advantage of the opportunity. The really horrible example of what could happen when soldiers decided to go home because their enlistments had expired did not occur in front of Boston, but far to the north, at Quebec, Canada.

For generations, the name Canada had meant danger to the people of New England and upper New York. Many Americans were afraid that the British would use Canada as a springboard for an attack upon the colonies. On the other hand, several influential colonial leaders fondly hoped that the people of Canada might feel as they did and that, if given a chance, Canada would join the thirteen colonies. An expedition was therefore planned to invade their neighbor to the north with a double purpose in mind: to forestall and prevent an advance of the British southward through the Hudson River Valley, and, if possible, to add a fourteenth colony to those already in revolt.

The American advance was to be made in two widely separated columns. The first column was to proceed northward from Fort Ticonderoga via Lake Champlain to attack Montreal; then it was to go eastward down the St. Lawrence to Quebec. This column was organized by Major General Philip Schuyler and his able second-in-command, Brigadier General Richard Montgomery. When Schuyler fell sick, the leadership of the expedition rested entirely upon the shoulders of Montgomery, who appears to have been almost the only one who had any real conception of the impracticality of the task involved. When he heard of the plan, he is said to have exclaimed, "A winter campaign in Canada! Posterity won't believe it!"

The second column was to go north through the Maine woods (then a part of Massachusetts) to join Montgomery in an attack upon Quebec. This column was commanded by Colonel Benedict Arnold, a man of intense energy, high courage, and driving ambition.

The whole idea of a march through this region was based primarily upon enthusiasm and ignorance. Furthermore, both expeditions were started so late in the year that winter would be sure to arrive before the mission could be accomplished. Although General Montgomery's column was opposed by a few scattered British troops and some Canadian militia, Colonel Arnold's men faced by far the more difficult task. The little force was to move from in front of Boston, sail across the water to the mouth of the Kennebec River, and then proceed northward. The difficulties encountered going upstream were far greater than anyone had expected, and the boats furnished them proved unserviceable. Nevertheless they kept going forward over thickly forested hills, across ice-cold marshes, facing dreary rain and high winds. Then as food supplies dwindled and storms lashed the little column, the faint-hearted among them turned back. The others kept marching bravely onward to encounter snow and bitterly cold sleet; their clothing was reduced to rags and tatters; and their food supply disappeared entirely. On November 9, 1775, after nearly two months of incredible suffering and hardship, 600 of the original 1,100 who had started reached the St. Lawrence opposite Quebec. It is remarkable, indeed, that there were any survivors of this historic march. Historians are generally agreed that, had it not been for the leadership qualities displayed by Colonel Arnold, by Captain Daniel Morgan, the commander of a company of riflemen, and by a few other courageous officers, all might have perished or turned back.

Four days later Montgomery entered Montreal; then with 300 men, he joined Arnold in front of Quebec. In the meantime Major General Guy Carleton, Military Governor of Canada, had reinforced the garrison so that there was little chance of capturing the city by assault. Then, to the horror of the American commanders, most of their men announced that they were going home on January 1 because their enlistments would be completed. In desperation, a night assault was organized and delivered on the last day of the year, the night before most of the men were to depart. It failed; Montgomery was killed, Arnold seriously wounded, and Morgan captured. The remnants of the American force remained under Arnold's command, in front of Quebec throughout the winter.

Of course the American leaders had known that most of their men were militia and that their enlistments were due to expire Yet it seemed incredible that true patriots would make that killing march to Quebec, then turn around and nullify all their efforts by going home. Even today, after nearly

200 years have passed, it makes no sense at all. It is completely illogical because these same men were willing to make that last desperate assault on Quebec the night before their enlistments ended. Then those who survived hastened homeward, leaving their outnumbered comrades to their fate.

Spurred on by the catastrophe at Quebec, Washington persisted in his efforts to create a Continental Army, but by mid-January he still had only half the number authorized. Another request therefore had to be made for militia to take the place of those who had been called in for the previous month.

This was certainly operating on a shoestring. Washington's own words in a letter to Congress dated February 9, 1776, illuminate the problems confronting him:

> The instance of General Montgomery (I mention it because it is a striking one, for a number of others might be adduced) proves that instead of having men to take advantage of circumstances you are in a manner compelled, right or wrong, to make circumstances yield to a secondary consideration. Since the 1st of December I have been devising every means in my power to secure these encampments; and though I am sensible that we never have since that period been able to act upon the offensive and at times not in a condition to defend, yet the cost of marching home one set of men, bringing in another, the havoc and waste occasioned by the first, the repairs necessary for the second, with a thousand incidental charges and inconveniences which have arisen and which it is scarce possible either to recollect or describe, amount to near as much as the keeping up a respectable body of troops the whole time ready for any emergency would have done.
>
> To this may be added that you never can have a well-disciplined army.
>
> To bring men to be well acquainted with the duties of a soldier requires time. To bring them under proper discipline and subordination not only requires time, but it is a work of great difficulty, and in this army, where there is so little distinction between the officers and soldiers, requires an uncommon degree of attention. To expect, then, the same service from raw and undisciplined

recruits as from veteran soldiers is to expect what never did and perhaps never will happen. Men who are familiarized to danger meet it without shrinking; whereas troops unused to service often apprehend danger where no danger is.

In this letter Washington described his difficulties with manpower. He did not dwell upon his supply shortages which were acute and distressing. One of the greatest of these problems, however, was being solved for him by a former bookseller from Boston named Henry Knox. The army had been trying to conduct a siege of Boston. It had established a line around the city but, because the army had no heavy cannon, it had been unable to do much more than stand and watch the British troops inside. Without artillery the Americans had no way of forcing an evacuation of the city.

Shortly after assuming command, Washington appointed Henry Knox as his chief of artillery. The new chief was eager to start to work, but without guns, there was little he could do. His thoughts turned toward Fort Ticonderoga, which had been captured from the British in May, 1775. He suggested to Washington that the cannon at the fort could be brought to Boston. Washington quickly agreed and ordered Knox to make the attempt. In mid-November he started forth. It is almost certain that Knox had no idea how difficult an undertaking he was about to attempt. The task required two months. It meant dragging guns through the snow in freezing weather, pulling them out when they fell through the ice, hauling them over mountains on poor or nonexistent roads, a distance of nearly 250 miles. Finally he reported to Washington with "a noble train of artillery." The commander-in-chief at last had the means to force an evacuation of the British.

Early in March, 1776, Washington seized Dorchester Heights overlooking the city of Boston from the south, emplaced his new artillery there, and quickly fortified the position. The American guns dominated the British shipping in the harbor. If Washington could not be driven from the heights, the British must evacuate the city. After one attempt to move against the position by water, which was prevented by a storm, the British commander decided to evacuate Boston. On March 17, Saint Patrick's Day, the British departed, taking the Loyalists and their families with them to Halifax, Nova Scotia.

A wave of rejoicing swept over the colonies. The proud British army had been humbled; it had been forced to leave the controversial city it had occupied for so long. The liberation of Boston was a great victory for the patriot cause, but to those who dared to look into the future, it was obvious that this could not be the end of the fighting. Neither King George III nor his ministers could let the colonies in rebellion win everything so easily. Furthermore, at this stage in the struggle it was not at all clear what sort of terms might be agreed upon by either side. The radical patriots wanted complete independence, but there had been no public declaration to that effect because many of those in revolt were not at all prepared for such a step at this time. They simply wanted to be granted the rights they thought all British subjects should have, particularly the right to govern themselves through their own elected assemblies. If the King and his ministers had been willing to grant the patriots these rights, with sufficient guarantees, the American Revolution might have been ended in its first year, with only the radicals unappeased.

Many of the leaders of the British Whigs, opposed to the Tories then in power in England, were sympathetic toward the American patriots. They were heartily in agreement with the principles for which the rebellious colonists were struggling, because they were trying to assert these same principles for the British people in England. In Parliament they supported the American point of view, but even the most forbearing of them could not have supported the idea of American independence. The colonies were too valuable to be lost completely. To further complicate the situation, a large segment of the population in America was not in revolt at all. Many were completely loyal to the crown and were ready to take up arms to fight alongside British troops. It has been estimated that only about half the people of the colonies were actively in favor of the war; the remainder were either indifferent to the outcome, or fought for the King. If all the people of the thirteen colonies had revolted it is hard to see how England with a population of about nine million could have had a chance of suppressing a revolution of two and one-half million people 3,000 miles away, when she had to provide garrisons for many other far-flung parts of her empire from India to Africa to Gibraltar, and also be prepared to face her ancient enemies, France and Spain.

With these considerations in mind many of the British leaders in America proved somewhat hesitant in their approach to the problem of rebellion, particularly if they had American connections or were members of the Whig party. A great deal of the British failure to act decisively can be explained by this one factor. For example, Lieutenant General Thomas Gage, the officer in command when the American Revolution began, had been on friendly terms with many Americans; his wife came from New Jersey, and he owned land in the colony of New York. His successor, General William Howe, who took command in October, 1775, was a Whig who had publicly announced that he would decline command of the armies in America because he was opposed to coercing the patriots. Of course, when ordered by the King to do so, he had obeyed the royal command. His attitude during the Siege of Boston was therefore predictable. Active campaigning would mean the use of force, which he wished to avoid, and which, if not successful, could drive many of those who had not yet taken sides into the rebel camp. Howe's army simply stayed inactive in Boston until forced to leave by the threat of bombardment from Dorchester Heights.

But the departure from Boston had been too humiliating. No officer commanding His Majesty's forces could let such a defeat end his career, which was a certainty if he did not take some aggressive action. By this time, also, the King's ministers had begun to realize that subjugation of the colonists in revolt would require a far greater effort than had originally been thought necessary.

Because the war was unpopular in England, and because large garrisons were also required at many other places in the British Empire, it had been difficult to raise enough troops to ensure success. To help solve this problem King George and his ministers decided to employ foreign mercenaries. This decision caused bitter resentment in the colonies, but, as a matter of fact, it was a perfectly normal procedure in Europe, a standard practice for hundreds of years. King George applied to Catherine the Great of Russia but she refused his request. He then obtained the men he wanted from some of the rulers of the various minor German states. Since the majority of these men came from Hesse-Cassel, they were known generally as Hessians. These soldiers certainly had not volunteered to be taken thousands of miles away from their country; they had been purchased and shipped abroad at a fixed amount per head, like so many cattle. They were resentful, homesick for Germany, and unable to speak English. However, since they were thoroughly trained and disciplined they followed orders, sometimes in brutal fashion, but they showed little enthusiasm or initiative because they had no interest in the war issues or the people involved in the struggle.

The British strategic plan for the year 1776 consisted of three parts. There were to be two attacks in the north and one in the south. The two northern advances were to constitute the main effort. They were to be directed toward either end of a long, almost uninterrupted waterway stretching from New York City up the Hudson River, thence via Lake Champlain to Canada. The object of these two attacks was to seize this line and cut New England off from the rest of the colonies. The British planners felt certain that, if the colonies in revolt could thus be divided into two parts, the rebellion would be crushed. In this assumption the planners were probably correct; however, it seemed advisable to them to make a secondary effort in the south also, to seize some of the major cities in that region and cooperate with the numerous Loyalists supposed to be operating there.

The three moves were not made simultaneously. The first, in point of time, was the northernmost. A large contingent of British and Hessian reinforcements landed in Canada in May. The outnumbered Americans besieging Quebec were forced to retreat, then easily defeated in a battle fought at Trois Rivières early in June, and pursued past Montreal southward toward Fort Ticonderoga.

The second British venture, aimed at the southern colonies, failed miserably. A poorly planned attack and a naval bombardment of Fort Sullivan on Sullivan's Island in the outer harbor of Charleston, South Carolina, on June 28 ended in an ignominious repulse. In commemoration of this exploit the fort was renamed Fort Moultrie, in honor of the American commander, Colonel William Moultrie, and the men who fought with him there. The fleet and the army transports sailed north to join the others already assembling for the third and largest invasion.

Where General Howe would make his attack was not too hard to guess. The largest seaport on the Atlantic coast was, of course, New York City, with a population, prior to the outbreak of hostilities, of 25,000, second only to Philadelphia, which numbered 40,000 and was one of the largest cities in the British Empire.

New York was so obviously Howe's next target that, on the very day after the liberation of Boston, Washington dispatched troops to New York to make preparations for its defense. In the latter part of June the British ships began to reach the scene. By mid-July over 300 warships and transports, including those from the ill-fated Charleston adventure, had anchored off Staten Island, just south of New York City. They had brought an army numbering 32,000 men. It was by far the largest,

27

most powerful force ever gathered together on the North American continent.

With this armada and with this army at their command, General William Howe and his brother, Vice Admiral Viscount Richard Howe, who was also a member of the Whig party, sought to negotiate with the patriots. In the meantime, however, the die had been cast; the Declaration of Independence had been signed on July 4. The Howes' peace offers were a waste of time because the King had given them power only to pardon; they had no authority to negotiate terms. Their intentions were of the best and, after the British capture of New York, meetings of commissioners were actually held but nothing concrete was ever accomplished.

From a military point of view the peace overtures put forth by the Howe brothers were extremely helpful to the American cause because each time they sought to negotiate they halted active operations against the Americans. Furthermore, whenever they won a battle, they failed to pursue to take full advantage of their victories. Apparently they were reluctant to shatter completely the forces under Washington, hoping that such halfway measures would cause less hard feeling in the future, when the colonists would again become loyal subjects of the Crown. It probably never occurred to either of them that there was the remotest chance the patriots would ever win this war; such a possibility was unthinkable. It was a good thing for the American cause that the Howes did not apply the basic military principle that Grant and Sherman demonstrated so effectively nearly ninety years later in the Civil War—first thoroughly defeat the enemy, then meet him on the friendliest possible terms.

Nearly two months passed before the British landed on Long Island, on August 22. The Battle of Long Island, or Brooklyn Heights, was fought on August 27. The result was a terrible defeat for the Americans. The only redeeming feature of the battle from the American point of view was the astonishing bravery, fortitude, and discipline shown by two

★NORTHERN THEATER OF WAR 1775-1776 ★

Quebec
Trois Rivières
CANADA
St. Lawrence R.
Montreal
St. Johns
VALCOUR IS.
Lake Champlain
Ft. Ticonderoga
Lake George
Mohawk R.
Albany
NEW YORK
Hudson R.
Delaware R.
PENN.
N.J.
Morristown
New Brunswick
Princeton
Trenton
Philadelphia
West Point
New York
LONG IS.
MASSACHUSETTS
CONN.
Concord
Lexington
Boston
Newport R.I.
NEW HAMPSHIRE
Kennebec R.
MAINE
(Part of MASS.)

Scale
0   30   60   90

J. Downey

NEW YORK & VICINITY
White Plains
Yonkers
Hudson R.
Ft. Lee
Ft. Wash.
Harlem Hgts.
MANHATTAN IS.
New York
Brooklyn
STATEN IS.
LONG IS.
Scale
0   5   10

29

Continental regiments, one from Maryland and one from Delaware. By their courage and ability these troops may have saved the American army on Long Island from complete annihilation on that day. General Howe failed to pursue and, two nights later, under cover of a thick mist, Washington, with the help of two Continental regiments composed of fishermen and sailors from Massachusetts, evacuated his men to New York City.

The escape from Long Island was a truly remarkable exploit. The British were amazed the following morning at daybreak to find only a deserted line of entrenchments. But the successful completion of the evacuation could not conceal from the public the seriousness of the defeat. Gloom was widespread and the militia began to depart for their homes in great numbers. In fact, the losses by desertion far exceeded those suffered in battle. General Washington used this opportunity to remind Congress again of the futility of relying upon militia, and stressed the absolute necessity of establishing a regular army that could be trusted to perform its duty.

In his letter he wrote: "Our situation is truly distressing. . . . The militia, instead of calling forth their utmost efforts to a brave and manly opposition in order to repair our losses, are dismayed, intractable, and impatient to return. Great numbers of them have gone off—in some instances almost by whole regiments, by half ones, and by companies at a time. . . . I am obliged to confess my want of confidence in the generality of the troops." Washington stated that "no dependence could be put in a militia." Earlier in the year he had suggested to the Congress that a bounty might encourage men to enlist. In June a bounty of ten dollars had been offered, but now Washington had discovered that the states were outbidding Congress. For in his same letter he added: "I can not find that the bounty of $10 is likely to produce the desired effect. When men can get double that sum to engage in the militia for a month or two . . . it is hardly to be expected."

He suggested that possibly "the addition of land might have a considerable influence on a permanent enlistment."

In England the King and his followers hailed the victory on Long Island with joy. General Howe was knighted for his achievement; the disgrace of losing Boston had been revenged. Two weeks later, on September 15, 1776, under cover of a naval bombardment, the British army landed on Manhattan Island and captured New York City. Then, on the next day, occurred the Battle of Harlem Heights, a small engagement, but one which came as an unpleasant surprise to the British and boosted American morale.

Untrained Americans, protected by entrenchments, had defended themselves bravely at Bunker Hill. Continental troops had fought magnificently at Long Island in a battle in the open, but they had, in the end, been forced to retreat. At Harlem Heights, for the first time, Americans saw the backs of their enemy. Continental soldiers from Connecticut and Virginia delivered a highly successful counterattack against some of the best units in the British Army. And, in an effort to raise the morale of his militia, Washington even brought into the fray those who had fled from the British landing force on the preceding day.

Harlem Heights was only a small affair but it proved to the many doubters that the British regular could be met in open warfare by trained American soldiers. Even the militia might do well under such conditions, if the Continentals were there to encourage them by their presence. And, by pure coincidence, on this day of battle, the Continental Congress resolved that "88 battalions be enlisted . . . to serve during the present war." On paper this looked fine. It provided for an army of about 60,000 men, but as long as the states persisted in their policy of bidding against the Continental Congress for recruits, a practice they continued to follow, this resolution could not begin to produce the army Washington so badly needed.

Five days after the Battle of Harlem Heights a great fire

31

broke out in New York. A large section was destroyed, perhaps as much as one-third of the city. Although it was undoubtedly accidental, each side accused the other of having started it. The immediate result was to make the British occupation problem much more difficult. They, and the Loyalists who had fled to New York to be under their protection, had expected to find comfortable homes and plenty of barracks space for the troops. Instead, everyone was crowded into less satisfactory quarters. The fire should have provided an additional incentive for General Howe to advance and secure more territory. It had the opposite effect: he used it as an excuse for additional delay.

While Washington and Howe had thus been struggling for possession of New York City, what, meanwhile, had happened to the British force that was supposed to come down from Canada? After forcing the Americans to return to Fort Ticonderoga, the point from which they had started their invasion of Canada ten months before, General Carleton had halted at St. Johns. Here he found it necessary to stop to assemble a fleet to operate on Lake Champlain. No large force could hope to penetrate the almost trackless forests of upper New York State without control of the waters of that lake.

General Schuyler, who supervised American operations in that theater, and General Gates in direct command of the troops, grasped this essential fact just as quickly. They placed Benedict Arnold, now a brigadier general, in charge of the construction and command of an American fleet, to be built with whatever material could be made available. There then ensued a shipbuilding race in which both sides exhibited extraordinary energy and resourcefulness.

From the beginning, however, Carleton had the advantage because he had some ships on the St. Lawrence, some of which he could dismantle and transport in pieces to St. Johns where they could be rebuilt. He also had far heavier guns at hand to mount on those ships. The result was the two-day naval Battle of Valcour Island. Arnold's little fleet was utterly destroyed, but the British advance was stopped. Carleton decided that since winter was so near he should not attempt a siege of Ticonderoga and turned back to St. Johns. The Americans, by building a fleet on Lake Champlain, thereby forcing the British to take the time to build a larger one, thus delayed the invasion of upper New York by a year. It may well be true that the year saved at Lake Champlain, for which the future traitor Benedict Arnold should be given the lion's share of the credit, saved the Revolution. For, if Carleton had seized Fort Ticonderoga, Burgoyne would have started from that point the next year, using it as a base for his supplies. With Lake Champlain firmly under his control, and with a much shorter distance to advance, Burgoyne might never have been stopped at Saratoga.

While this eventful naval battle was being fought, General Howe finally moved forward. His first landing on a peninsula in lower New York was a failure, but the second landing was more successful. When Howe's army marched northward toward White Plains, General Washington was forced to withdraw from Manhattan Island. On October 28, the Battle of White Plains was fought. Only a portion of each army was engaged; Washington retreated farther northward to a better position to await attack.

At this point General Howe turned back. It was pointless to continue this pursuit with no definite objective in mind, and he had become aware of a terrible blunder made by his enemies. When the American forces evacuated Manhattan Island they had left behind a large garrison to hold Fort Washington and Fort Lee across the river on the New Jersey shore. On November 16, the British and Hessians stormed Fort Washington; over 2,600 prisoners were captured. Four days later Fort Lee fell. Although the garrison escaped, more guns and ammunition were irretrievably lost. General Howe began a swift advance across New Jersey toward Philadelphia.

Back in September, eight days after the Battle of Harlem Heights, Washington had written to Congress: "We are now, as it were, upon the eve of another dissolution of our Army. The remembrance of the difficulties which happened upon the occasion last year, and the consequences which might have followed the change if proper advantages had been taken by the enemy . . . afford but a very gloomy prospect in the appearance of things now." When he wrote that letter, the commander-in-chief was thinking primarily of the fact that his men's enlistments were again due to expire at the end of the year, and he would again be left without an army. Now, in November, the situation was far worse than he had ever visualized back in September. It began to look as if his army would disappear before the enlistments were over.

As the remnants withdrew across the Delaware into Pennsylvania, the American cause was indeed at a low ebb. Two things conspired to save that cause: Washington's indomitable will to win and Howe's decision that the war, for all practical purposes, had already been won. It is simple today to criticize the British commander for not continuing the pursuit of his defeated enemy until the entire patriot army had been destroyed. But it is just as easy to see why he thought he could stop and let the Continental Army dissolve of its own accord. Fort Washington had been captured, together with its entire garrison, with comparative ease. The pursuit across New Jersey had been such a complete succss that, for the first time, he was beginning to get results from his peace feelers. A large number of people, heretofore unwilling to take sides in the war, had elected to take an oath of loyalty to the British crown. His enemy's retreating army had become so depleted in strength that General Howe felt no hesitation whatever in deciding to send a large force from New York to capture Newport, Rhode Island. The remainder of his British and Hessian force encountered no difficulty in continuing its pursuit. Howe therefore decided to call a halt and go into winter quarters. He felt certain that, with such an unpromising future, Washington would be able to obtain very few men to take the place of those whose enlistments would expire on January 1.

Washington saw just as clearly as General Howe that the American cause needed a victory, or it would die as soon as the new year came. He had received a few reinforcements. With these added to his trusted, but weary and worn Continentals, he felt that he had barely enough men on hand to attempt a desperate counterstroke. On midafternoon of Christmas Day he set his men in motion toward the Delaware River, to cross that night and make an attack on the Hessian troops quartered in Trenton, New Jersey. The result was such a complete surprise that the Battle of Trenton was probably the most one-sided battle in the history of warfare.

Next came the Battle of Princeton on January 3, 1777. By this time the enlistments of many of the Continentals had expired, but some had been persuaded to remain an extra month or six weeks by the promise of a bounty. It was most fortunate that they were present, for this battle was not so one-sided. At a very critical moment the American line gave way, but the presence of Washington himself and the opportune arrival of additional Continental troops saved the day. Shortly thereafter the American army went into winter quarters at Morristown.

By the brilliant, decisive counterstrokes at Trenton and Princeton the American cause was saved. A measure of confidence returned to those who had begun to despair. Yet the Continental Army, which had saved that cause, had practically disappeared. Shortly after the Battle of Princeton, Washington informed the President of Congress that he was in the position "of scarce having any army at all." Even two months later, when a few soldiers had arrived in response to his earnest entreaties for reinforcements, he reported his effective strength as less than 3,000 men: "These, 981 excepted, are militia and stand engaged only till the last of this month."

Then, slowly, men began to come into camp in greater numbers. By the latter half of May, 1777, there were about 8,000 men enlisted in the Continental service. And, at last, these soldiers were to serve for longer periods than a year.

They were now enlisted for three years, or for the duration of the war.

By this time, also, the authorized strength of the Continental Army had been increased. Near the end of December, 1776, during the Trenton-Princeton crisis, the Continental Congress had vested Washington with dictatorial powers for six months, and authorized him to raise a force totaling about 75,000 men. This remained the strength (on paper) for four years, when it was reduced in order to conform a bit more closely to reality. For at no time did the actual strength of the Continental Army even approximate the allotted numbers. The units were always understrength. Battle and disease took their toll. More men were always needed to take the place of the casualties, and eventually to replace those whose three-year enlistments had expired.

Throughout the remainder of the war Washington and his officers were continuously faced with these same discouraging problems, for which no solution could be found. The army never was maintained at a reasonable strength. The pattern had already been set. Militia service close to home, for shorter periods of time, with more frequent bounties, continued to be far more attractive.

2

"Gentleman Johnny" Plans to Win the War

Washington was perplexed—and well he might be. At last he had an army of over 8,000 men, most of them enlisted for three years. Although the majority were recruits, a large number, including several of the officers and noncommissioned officers, had seen service in 1775 and 1776. Given sufficient time, Washington could hope that the army could be developed into an efficient fighting machine, capable of facing the best that the British Army could bring into the field.

The big questions were: would time be given him to prepare his new Continental Army for battle; and what were the British plans for the year 1777? In May, a strong army of British and Hessians, with some Canadians and Indians, had begun assembling in Canada. Would these be sent by water down to New York, or would they move southward by way of Lake Champlain toward the Hudson? If the enemy concentrated at New York City, a pitched battle might be fought near there, possibly in New Jersey. Washington would have to call on General Philip Schuyler to send him all his Continentals from upper New York, which were very few in number. The British and Hessians would surely be far stronger than the Continental Army; it was a very unattractive prospect.

If, on the other hand, the enemy in Canada were to move via Lake Champlain, the British in New York would certainly advance up the Hudson to meet them. This would mean defending both ends of the river against superior numbers. If this was the British plan the American army in Morristown, New Jersey, was not in the proper place. It was well sited to

37

guard against an overland advance against Philadelphia, such as General Howe had undertaken the previous year, but the army was completely out of position to defend the line of the Hudson.

As news filtered into his headquarters during the month of May, the American commander-in-chief was able to deduce that the British in Canada were preparing to move southward through New York State, but General Howe was making no move to cooperate with the northern army. Instead there developed, during the last days of May and most of the month of June, a series of apparently aimless maneuvers in New Jersey. Perhaps General Howe was trying to see how much opposition might be encountered if an overland march were undertaken against Philadelphia, although such a move would be counter to all the rules of logic, warfare, and common sense. Later, General Howe was to explain that the purpose of these operations had been to try to tempt Washington into giving battle. Naturally the Americans had not risen to the bait because they were by no means ready for a real battle on a large scale against an army which outnumbered them.

The June campaigning in New Jersey had been excellent experience for the new Continental Army. Also, a few more recruits had come to swell the American ranks. In effect, Sir William Howe had handed to Washington a whole month's time to increase the strength of his army and further its combat efficiency. Then at the end of the month, the British and Hessians evacuated New Jersey, transferring all their troops to Staten Island and New York, leaving Washington still in doubt as to their future plans. There was, however, no question at all as to the intentions of the army that had been assembled in Canada. On July 1, it landed just north of Fort Ticonderoga and began operations against that fortress.

The British strategic plan for the year 1777 had been developed in a peculiar manner. It was not the product of General Howe, the commander-in-chief in New York, nor had it been initiated by the King or his principal war advisors, although they had agreed to it. The plan had been prepared by an ambitious major general who had seen some service in this war, but to date he had always been in a secondary position, which was irritating because it brought him no honors, fame, or reputation.

Major General John Burgoyne was not a typical product of the British Army. After a brief period of service lasting only three years, he had resigned his commission. Nine years later, when the Seven Years' War broke out, he had returned to active duty as a captain. During that war he had served with distinction, had been promoted, and then had been elected a member of Parliament. Being both a soldier and a politician was not unusual in those days, but Burgoyne also aspired to fame as a wit and playwright. In fashionable eighteenth-century English society this combination had probably helped his military advancement. Certainly it had brought him to the attention of higher authority in an age where drawing room politics was almost essential to a successful career. One of his plays had been performed in London and had been fairly successful, although his style of writing was a bit too flamboyant even for the people of that era who were accustomed to flowery speeches. In America his love for majestic wording would prove harmful.

After professing a lack of enthusiasm for the conflict, Burgoyne had arrived in Boston in May, 1775, aboard the same ship which carried Generals Howe and Clinton. Upon arrival, he was shocked to discover that, a month after the Battles of Lexington and Concord, the British were practically besieged in Boston. Then came the Battle of Bunker Hill, in which he took no part, but did watch from a hill in Boston. From this experience he learned the obvious lesson that a direct assault should not be made upon Americans sheltered by fortifications, but this seems to have been about the only lesson that he did learn during his service in America in 1775 and 1776.

In December, 1775, General Burgoyne returned to England,

and was then sent to Canada in command of the British and Hessian reinforcements which arrived at Quebec in May, 1776. During the campaign which followed, ending at Valcour Island in October, he served simply as second-in-command to General Carleton. This year's experience should have been excellent training. Burgoyne should have spent all his leisure time learning about conditions in America, the people who lived in the colonies, and the problems of warfare in such a sparsely settled, wooded country. General Carleton, an able, understanding administrator and an excellent soldier, would have made a superb teacher, from whom he could have learned a great deal.

Instead, Burgoyne seems to have spent most of his time fretting because he was only second-in-command. At the end of the campaign he left Canada for England, determined to use all his influence to obtain for himself a more prominent position. He arrived at a very opportune moment. King George III, his Prime Minister, Lord Frederick North, and Lord George Germain, the Colonial Secretary, were all angry at General Carleton for having stopped his advance after the Battle of Valcour Island. For a while it appeared that Burgoyne might share the blame for the failure to capture Fort Ticonderoga, but this did not last long. Germain and Carleton had been bitter enemies for many years. Soon Germain realized that it would be to his own advantage in his quarrel with Carleton to place all the blame on his personal enemy. He therefore supported the plan that Burgoyne then proposed for the winning of the Revolution in 1777, and the King's approval was obtained.

In many ways the Burgoyne plan was simply a repetition of the 1776 plan to gain control of Lake Champlain and the Hudson River, thus severing New England from the rest of the colonies. General Howe was to advance northward from New York while a large force moved southward from Canada through Albany to meet him. The commander of the northern army was not specifically designated in the plan but the choice was obvious. For political reasons Carleton could not be selected; therefore, King George graciously indicated that Burgoyne should be promoted to lieutenant general and placed in direct charge of the expedition. Germain's personal enemy, Sir Guy Carleton, was relegated to a minor role, that of simply providing all possible assistance. The Colonial Secretary then joyfully wrote a letter to his enemy informing him in a very insulting manner of the part he was to play in the British plan. Like a good soldier, Carleton expressed his views, then swallowed his pride and proceeded to follow orders. In the campaign that followed there would be no valid criticism of his performance of his assigned duty.

As for the plan itself, it had one outstanding virtue over that conceived for the previous year. There was to be no diversion of regular soldiers or fleet units on any secondary venture, such as that directed toward Charleston, South Carolina, in 1776. Nothing was to interfere with the principal objective—the meeting of Howe's and Burgoyne's armies on the Hudson River after Burgoyne captured Albany.

In the light of what actually occurred, it might seem curious that Burgoyne believed that he would reach Albany without any help from General Howe. Apparently the planners did not expect to find any real opposition until they met Washington's Continental Army, which, they assumed, would then be caught as in the jaws of a vise between Burgoyne and Howe, moving northward from New York. The British planners realized, at least dimly, what Washington and his generals had learned: that there were two types of soldiers in the American forces. The Battles of Brooklyn Heights, Harlem Heights, Trenton, and Princeton had taught the British a certain amount of respect for the Continentals, who could be relied upon to stand and fight. Their training and equipment were not yet on a par with the British regular; for example, only a few were equipped with bayonets or knew how to use them. But these soldiers would not run home when the going got tough. The Continentals must be defeated on the field of

41

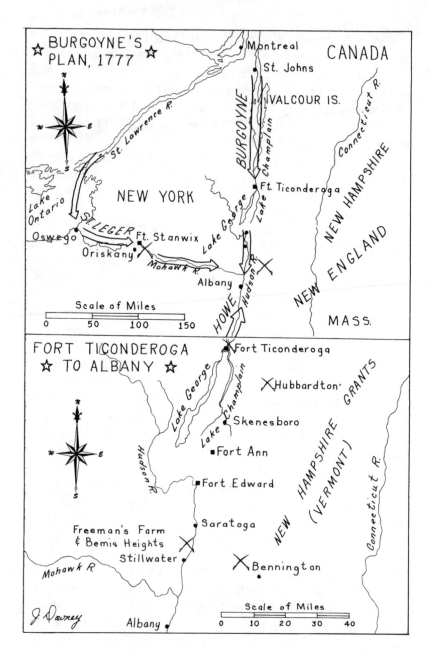

BURGOYNE'S
PLAN, 1777

Montreal
St. Johns
CANADA

N
W E
S

BURGOYNE

VALCOUR IS.

St. Lawrence R.

Lake Champlain

Connecticut R.

Lake Ontario

NEW YORK

Ft. Ticonderoga

Lake George

NEW HAMPSHIRE

ST. LEGER

Oswego

Ft. Stanwix

Oriskany

Mohawk R.

Lake George

Albany

Hudson R.

NEW ENGLAND

Scale of Miles

0   50   100   150

HOWE

MASS.

FORT TICONDEROGA
☆ TO ALBANY ☆

Fort Ticonderoga

Hubbardton

N
W E
S

Lake George

Lake Champlain

Skenesboro

Hudson R.

Fort Ann

Fort Edward

Saratoga

NEW HAMPSHIRE GRANTS

Connecticut R.

Freeman's Farm
& Bemis Heights

Stillwater

Bennington

(VERMONT)

Mohawk R.

J. Downey

Albany

Scale of Miles

0   10   20   30   40

42

battle before the American revolt would collapse. There were only a few of these soldiers at Fort Ticonderoga, and they would be so outnumbered that the planners assumed the big battle would not occur until after Albany had been reached and Washington's army encountered. Then, together, Howe and Burgoyne would bring the Revolution to a successful conclusion.

The second type of soldier in the American forces was, of course, the militiaman. Burgoyne had witnessed the defense of Bunker Hill. He resolved not to repeat such an obvious costly mistake but, for every other practical purpose, the militiamen were ignored. It never seemed to occur to him that the militia might prove helpful to the American cause in many other ways, not on the field of battle. That they could delay his army, snipe at it in his camps, and even surround and destroy isolated detachments never was considered. The possibility that his army might be whittled down to a small enough size so that it would eventually be forced to fight a battle on equal terms with an equivalent number of Continental soldiers certainly never entered Burgoyne's mind.

Nothing more clearly illustrates the British planners' failure to understand the opposition to be encountered than their provision for a third column to take part in this campaign. It was to be under the command of Lieutenant Colonel Barry St. Leger, promoted for the duration to the temporary rank of brigadier general. The expedition was to be composed of a mixture of whites and Indians in approximately equal numbers. Since there were only a few regulars involved, Burgoyne probably did not consider this a diversion in the same category as the Charleston expedition of the preceding year. The majority of the white men were Tories. There were some Canadians, and several hundred Indians. St. Leger was to proceed up the St. Lawrence, across Lake Ontario to Oswego where the Indians were to be met, thence by way of the Mohawk Valley to Albany. To think that only 900 white men and about 900 Indians could force their way from Oswego to

Albany nearly 200 miles without encountering substantial opposition shows complete ignorance of the country and the people. Admittedly, some of the population were Loyalist in sentiment, but the presence of the Indians would be sure to sway all brave men, who were wavering in their sentiment, to the colonial cause. To protect their families from Indian outrages they would have to fight on the side of the patriots.

Burgoyne would have been well advised to have omitted the St. Leger column from his plan. It was too small a force to reach its objective, or affect the outcome on the Hudson. As it proceeded, it engendered its own opposition. Very few of the Americans who rose to the defense of their homes in the Mohawk Valley would have gone to join their countrymen on the Hudson. They would not have dared to leave their valley completely unprotected, for Tories and Indians to raid at will. The fighting that occurred in the Mohawk Valley was thus primarily a struggle between the New York settlers and their Tory equivalents, aided by Indian allies. The few Continental soldiers who appeared on the scene were approximately equal in numbers to the British and German regulars who opposed them. Thus the St. Leger column had no practical effect upon the outcome of Burgoyne's expedition. It did not, except for a very brief space of time, affect the balance of power on the Hudson. The British supplies sent to St. Leger might, on the other hand, have been very helpful to Burgoyne.

Another excellent illustration of Burgoyne's total inability to understand the American colonists occurred just prior to his landing near Fort Ticonderoga. He issued a proclamation addressed to the people of the colonies, accusing the patriots of all sorts of crimes, offering encouragement to the Loyalists, and then threatening dire consequences to those who remained in revolt. It is a remarkable document, a wonderful example of Burgoyne the dramatist at his very worst. Nothing could have been more poorly adapted to the taste of the people for whom it was designed:

"Gentleman Johnny" Plans to Win the War

By John Burgoyne, Esq., Lieutenant-General of his Majesty's armies in America . . .

The forces entrusted to my command are designed to act in concert, and upon a common principle, with the numerous armies and fleets which already display in every quarter of America, the power, the justice, and when properly sought, the mercy of the King.

The cause in which the British arms are thus exerted, applies to the most affecting interests of the human heart. . . . To the eyes and ears of the temperate part of the public, and to the breasts of suffering thousands in the provinces, be the melancholy appeal, whether the present unnatural rebellion has not been made a foundation for the completest system of tyranny that ever God, in his displeasure, suffered for a time to be exercised over a forward and stubborn generation.

Arbitrary imprisonment, confiscation of property, persecution and torture, unprecedented in the inquisitions of the Romish church, are among the palpable enormities that verify the affirmative. These are inflicted by assemblies and committees, who dare to profess themselves friends to liberty, upon the most quiet subjects, without distinction of age or sex, for the sole crime, often for the sole suspicion, of having adhered in principle to the government under which they were born. . . .

The intention of this address is to hold forth security, not depredation to the country. To those whom spirit and principle may induce to partake of the glorious task of redeeming their countrymen from dungeons, and re-establishing the blessings of legal government, I offer encouragement and employment. . . . The domestic, the industrious, the infirm, and even the timid inhabitants, I am desirous to protect, provided they remain quietly at their houses; that they do not suffer their cattle to be removed, nor their corn or forage to be secreted or destroyed; that they do not break up their bridges or roads; nor by any other act, directly or indirectly, endeavor to obstruct the operations of the King's troops, or supply or assist those of the enemy. Every species of provision brought to my camp, will be paid for at an equitable rate, and in solid coin.

In consciousness of Christianity, my royal master's clemency, and the honor of soldiership, I have dwelt upon this invitation

. . . and let not people be led to disregard it, by considering their distance from the immediate situation of my camp. I have but to give stretch to the Indian forces under my direction, and they amount to thousands, to overtake the hardened enemies of Great Britain and America. . . .

If, notwithstanding these endeavors . . . the frenzy of hostility should remain, I trust I shall stand acquitted in the eyes of God and men in denouncing and executing the vengeance of the State against the wilful outcasts. The messengers of justice and of wrath await them in the field; and devastation, famine, and every concomitant horror. . . .

Then, to make matters worse, Burgoyne made a flowery speech to his Indians telling them to make war in a civilized manner. The combination of his proclamation, threatening to use thousands of Indians, and this speech, asking his red allies to obey the rules of war, was too much for the good people of America. At first they were astounded and shocked; then their sense of humor got the better of them. In the end Burgoyne became an object of laughter and ridicule, not only in America, but also 3,000 miles away in the House of Commons in London. There was, however, a difference in the type of laughter evoked in London and the type produced in New York and New England. It was all right to make fun of Burgoyne so long as his expedition did not advance far enough to be dangerous to the safety of home and family. If that occurred something would have to be done to stop him.

General Burgoyne had assembled an army of 7,850 men on Lake Champlain. Over 4,100 of these were British regulars; nearly 3,100 were German soldiers; there were 150 Canadians, 100 Tories, and some 400 Indians. Except for the Canadians, Tories, and Indians, it was a well-equipped, superbly trained and disciplined body of men, ready and eager to go into battle. Furthermore, they had learned to trust their leader who had shown himself to be thoughtful and considerate of their needs. In this respect Burgoyne was way ahead of his time. He did not believe in cruel punishments, tried to treat his soldiers like human beings, and teach them their trade by inspiration rather than by brute force. He insisted that his officers educate themselves thoroughly on all subjects dealing with their profession. As a result the men under his command were more efficient than most and showed an unusual amount of initiative. The British soldier's nickname for Burgoyne, "Gentleman Johnny," was meant to be respectful, although the Americans, not realizing how highly his men regarded him and remembering his unfortunate proclamation, treated the nickname as a joke.

Late in June, the army and the British fleet advanced southward up Lake Champlain. On July 1, they landed just north of Fort Ticonderoga, expecting to encounter strong resistance. This was the most famous fortress in North America. Originally built by the French it had played a prominent part in the French and Indian War, and then had been allowed to fall into a state of decay. In the last year, however, the Americans had made an effort to strengthen its defenses but the fort, together with its outlying works, had been designed for a much larger garrison than the Americans had provided. The American commander, Major General Arthur St. Clair, had only about 3,400 men at his disposal. Furthermore, the main fort was dominated by a high hill named Sugar Loaf, a mile to the southwest, which was not fortified. General Horatio Gates, who had appointed St. Clair to command this fortress, had decided several months before that this hill was inaccessible and that no time or effort should be wasted on it.

After capturing St. Clair's principal outpost on the west shore of the lake, "Gentleman Johnny" took a look at Sugar Loaf. Summoning an engineer lieutenant, he sent him to make a personal reconnaissance. The lieutenant returned confident that he could build a road and that guns could be emplaced at the top within twenty-four hours. Burgoyne assigned the problem to Major General William Phillips, his able second-in-command, who was a fine artilleryman.

On the morning of July 5, St. Clair looked up to the top

of Sugar Loaf and there discovered two artillery pieces being mounted in place. Soon they would be firing directly down upon him. The American commander wisely decided to evacuate his post. That night he crossed over to the eastern shore of Lake Champlain, sending some artillery and supplies by water to Skenesboro (now Whitehall). A number of cannon and other matériel had to be abandoned.

About daybreak the British began a vigorous pursuit. The fleet caught up with the waterborne elements just after they had disembarked at Skenesboro. To prevent supplies from falling into British hands, the Americans destroyed everything that would burn including all but two of their ships, and then escaped to Fort Ann. The two ships were captured.

On the next day the pursuers, marching eastward from Ticonderoga, fought a fierce battle with St. Clair's rear guard at Hubbardton (Vermont). On this day the British and Hessians got a good taste of what might be in store for them in the future because St. Clair had put some of his best troops with the rear guard, most of them Continental infantry. Casualties were heavy on both sides. In the end the British held the field but the pursuit was halted. The rest of St. Clair's men escaped and, by a circuitous route, rejoined the army at Fort Edward, New York.

The fall of Fort Ticonderoga was a stupendous shock to the colonists. Its reputation acquired during the French and Indian War had been so great that it had come to be regarded as comparable in strength to Gibraltar. King George III and his favorite ministers hailed its capture with joy and thought the Revolution was now practically crushed.

At this moment, in his hour of victory, Burgoyne made the biggest mistake of his entire career. The decision to send St. Leger into the Mohawk Valley, the later dispatch of a poorly planned expedition to Bennington, his future battlefield mistakes at Freeman's Farm and at Bemis Heights all pale into comparative insignificance beside the monumental error that Burgoyne now made. There were two possible ways to reach the Hudson River from Skenesboro. One was to plunge straight through the forest along a narrow road to Fort Ann, thence to Fort Edward, a distance of twenty-three miles. The practical difficulties presented along this route were obvious. The road would have to be widened to take a large quantity of supplies, and a certain amount of bridging would be necessary for wagons to pass over the small streams that would be encountered.

The other route involved returning to Fort Ticonderoga, and then getting boats from Lake Champlain across into Lake George. It was impossible for boats to fight their way through the gorge and over the falls and rapids connecting the two lakes. A portage of about three miles would therefore be necessary but, once that obstacle had been overcome, it would be clear sailing up the lake to where a good road led to the Hudson only ten miles away.

Burgoyne decided to use the route through the forest for his army; but then he sent his boats, his artillery, and other heavy equipment over the portage to Lake George. Apparently the prime factor in his decision to push straight through the wilderness was that he did not wish to appear to be retreating, and a return to Ticonderoga could give that impression. Perhaps he recalled all the censure that had been heaped upon General Carleton when that officer turned back after Valcour Island. At any rate, when he made his decision, General Burgoyne seems to have given no consideration as to which of the two routes could be more easily, or more effectively, obstructed by the colonials.

"Gentlemen Johnny" had a very clear understanding of the manner in which his own soldiers would react in any given situation, but he misjudged his enemies every time. His proclamation at the beginning of the campaign, when he tried to frighten the patriots into submission, is clear evidence of his inability to understand the people whom he expected to subdue.

The prompt and easy capture of Ticonderoga alarmed the

people of New York and New England, but instead of rushing to Burgoyne's camp to declare their loyalty to their King, a large number of volunteers began leaving their homes to join the fight against the invader. General Philip Schuyler, the commander of the American army, knew these men were not trained for warfare and therefore put them to work felling trees across the road to Fort Edward. They destroyed every bridge across every creek and also turned parts of the road into swamps by diverting streams. Schuyler adopted a scorched earth policy. He persuaded the inhabitants to drive away their cattle and horses, and even burn their crops.

The result was extremely effective. It took Burgoyne's men three weeks to reach Fort Edward, which may be calculated as an average rate of advance of one mile per day. As a matter of fact it was a remarkable achievement to have made that much progress through the obstacles that Schuyler's men put in their path. The soldiers, when they reached Fort Edward on July 29, congratulated themselves on the success of their advance, but not so Burgoyne. He was at last beginning to have doubts of his ultimate success. This slow hacking through the forest didn't remotely resemble the triumphal march he had expected after the capture of Fort Ticonderoga. These Americans baffled him. Instead of flocking to greet him, or at least waiting to welcome his troops, they had combined to place every possible obstacle in his path. They were doing him as much harm as if they were capable of defeating his army in battle. At this rate, unless he could speed his progress, he would need more supplies than he had thought necessary. And the time that had been lost was appalling. He should have been in Albany already; had he taken the other route he probably would have been there by now.

Five days after his arrival at Fort Edward on the Hudson, Burgoyne received a stunning shock. He learned that General Howe was not moving up the river to join forces with him somewhere near Albany, but was enroute to Philadelphia to capture the colonial capital. The largest British army on the continent, the one which was supposed to ensure the success of his plan, had gone in the wrong direction, headed south instead of north.

Now Burgoyne really began to worry. He thought of turning back but couldn't bring himself to face that idea yet. Furthermore he had heard nothing recently from St. Leger for whose fate he was entirely responsible. He could not desert his comrades, as Howe had deserted him. Burgoyne felt that he must press on but, before he did so, why not do something to help his supply situation? The future was getting more uncertain all the time and there was no telling how long his campaign might last. He had been told that, in the Connecticut Valley to the east, supplies were abundant and that a number of horses could also he obtained; these he particularly needed.

An expedition was therefore organized to obtain these supplies. The composition of the troops involved was peculiar to say the least. The officer entrusted with the command was Lieutenant Colonel Friedrich Baum, a German officer who could not speak a word of English. For a separate detachment to operate independently this was certainly an unusual choice, especially since one of his missions was to enlist the services of the English-speaking people in the district. He was given 300 Germans and about 50 British soldiers.

Then some 300 Tories, Canadians, and Indians were placed under his command. It might be noted here that Burgoyne again and again made the same mistake, of sending too few men to perform an important mission. First, he provided St. Leger with an entirely inadequate force for his long march down the Mohawk Valley; here he allotted Colonel Baum only 650 men, and we shall see how he used only a part of his army at Freeman's Farm, and brought disaster upon himself at Bemis Heights by sending out only a portion of his army.

The detachment began its march on August 11, but it was not very long until Colonel Baum realized that the chances were excellent that he would have to face a far larger number of men than he had expected. He promptly sent back to Burgoyne for additional troops. Another column of 650 Germans commanded by Lieutenant Colonel Heinrich von Breymann was dispatched to support him. It was very slow in moving and did not arrive until the afternoon of the day of battle, August 16, by which time it was too late. Colonel Baum was left to face the enemy with what he had on hand, which, by this time, amounted to 800 men; another 150 Tories had joined him while he was on the march.

The commander of the opposing American force was John Stark who, in this emergency, had been commissioned a brigadier general by the State of New Hampshire. Here was a veteran soldier who had seen service in the French and Indian War and fought at Bunker Hill and at the Battles of Trenton and Princeton. For about a month he had been gathering men to defend his state. He was extremely popular and highly respected; volunteers had come eagerly to serve under his command so that, at the beginning of the battle, he had collected a force of some 2,000 militia. An additional unit, Continentals from the future State of Vermont (the Green Mountain Boys,) commanded by Colonel Seth Warner, another very popular officer, was enroute to join him. Like Colonel von Breymann's troops, they did not arrive until late in the afternoon.

This is the battle that comes the closest to fulfilling the popular concept that, in the American Revolution, untrained Americans led by amateur generals defeated the regular soldiers of Europe. It is the battle to which orators most often point with pride but, surely, in doing so, it cannot be claimed that John Stark was, at this time, an amateur general.

In any event, the Battle of Bennington should be considered carefully, although it is not necessary to describe in detail how it was fought. With his 2,000 men, General Stark attacked. The Canadians and Indians fled as soon as they heard gunfire. Most of the Tories ran as rapidly, after firing one volley. This left Colonel Baum with something over 350 men surrounded by 2,000, odds of over five to one. At this point, whether the militia were trained to fight or not, the British and Germans were certain of defeat. Yet they clung to their position until their ammunition ran low, and then charged into the Americans surrounding them, finally surrendering when their leader, Colonel Baum, fell mortally wounded.

It is odd that those who like to dwell upon the Battle of Bennington as the battle where untrained militia fought so well against disciplined soldiers do not pay more attention to the second part of the battle. As soon as Colonel Baum's Canadians, Tories, and Indians fled, leaving him outnumbered five to one, his troops had no chance at all of winning. However, Colonel von Breymann's reinforcing column of 650 men had a much better chance of success. When his soldiers appeared, the Americans were scattered over the field gathering the spoils of victory. General Stark and Colonel Warner, who had arrived in advance of his regiment, hastily gathered men together, tried to make a stand, but were forced to retreat. Fortunately Colonel Warner's Continental regiment then reached the field. Steadied by their presence, the retreating Americans turned again to face the enemy. At this point von Breymann's Germans were running low on ammunition; he ordered a retreat. The Americans undertook a vigorous pursuit until dark. In this second part of the battle it is impracticable to calculate the odds as closely as in the first phase involving Baum's command. It is probable that here the Americans outnumbered their enemy only about three to one.

The Battle of Bennington was a terrible blow to Burgoyne. On that day his army lost about 900 killed, wounded, missing, and captured. Shortly afterward the British general was given some more dreadful news. St. Leger's Mohawk Valley expedition had turned back. The campaign had begun with a siege of Fort Stanwix, bravely defended by a mixed force of Continentals and militia commanded by Colonel Peter Gansevoort. Then a relief expedition led by Brigadier General Nicholas Herkimer was ambushed on August 6, near Oriskany, six miles from the fort. The battle that resulted was perhaps the most desperate, hand-to-hand struggle, with tomahawks, clubbed muskets, and knives, ever fought on the American continent. The Loyalists and Indians retreated but the Americans were unable to pursue. They also retreated, carrying the mortally wounded Herkimer with them. The siege continued until Major General Benedict Arnold was sent by General Schuyler with another relief expedition. For once in his life Arnold avoided a fight. A half-witted German and an Oneida Indian were sent to St. Leger's camp with the news that Arnold was coming with thousands of men. The Indians treated the half-wit with the respect they always gave insane people, believed his story about Arnold, whom they feared, and panicked at the news. St. Leger had no choice but to retreat.

At this point "Gentleman Johnny" should have turned back, at least as far as Fort Ticonderoga. He could have easily retreated by way of Lake George and saved his army, though not his reputation. There was no further obligation to remain to help St. Leger in case he should appear. Too many men had been lost at Bennington. The army was not yet defeated in battle but more Continental regiments were on their way, sent by Washington. Although this fact may not have been known by Burgoyne, it was always a possibility.

Furthermore, the countryside was rising against him in greater numbers than ever before, encouraged by news of the Bennington victory, and alarmed by one of the most intelligent pieces of propaganda ever utilized in warfare. Two days before the British and German army had reached Fort Edward, a party of Indians had captured, shot, and scalped a young woman named Jane McCrea. She had been engaged to be married to an officer in Burgoyne's army. News of the murder was spread far and wide, emphasizing the obvious fact that even those under the protection of the British Crown were not safe from these marauding savages. It was wonderful propaganda and the American leaders made the most of it. Her name and fate became known throughout the land; volunteers came pouring into the American camp.

Word also spread through New England that a new commander had been appointed by the Continental Congress to take the place of General Schuyler. The people from the New England states had never liked Schuyler. He was a representative of the New York aristocracy, which they distrusted on general principles. Although he had performed remarkably fine service delaying the advance of the enemy to Fort Edward, they blamed him and St. Clair for the loss of Fort Ticonderoga, which was, of course, grossly unfair. Many had even objected to his sending Arnold to the relief of Fort Stanwix because it would weaken the force opposed to Burgoyne. It was therefore welcome news to New Englanders that General Horatio Gates had been chosen by the Congress to take Schuyler's place. Gates was popular in New England. The combination of the news of Bennington, the terrible story of the murder of Jane McCrea, and the fact that Schuyler had been replaced by Gates caused thousands of men to volunteer for service in the army facing Burgoyne.

Confronted by this rising tide of opposition, fearful of sending out another independent detachment which might meet the same fate as that of Colonel Baum's force, General Burgoyne waited in place until he could accumulate the necessary transport, equipment, and supplies for another move southward toward Albany. This meant nearly a month's delay, for everything he needed must now come by the long route from Canada. During this waiting period the spotlight of activity shifted to focus on the operations of the larger armies of Washington and Howe.

3

General Howe Encounters Unexpected Resistance

On July 3, 1777, the day that General Burgoyne's engineer officer was climbing Sugar Loaf to see if it might be the key to the capture of Fort Ticonderoga, General Sir William Howe started to load his army onto the transports that would take them away from New York City, southward toward Philadelphia. Six days later the embarkation was complete. Then for two weeks, while Burgoyne's army was cutting its way through the forest, Howe's troops lay sweltering in the burning sun on board the transports, waiting for favorable winds. Thus, while Burgoyne was engaged in the execution of his fatal decision to take the wrong road to reach the Hudson, General Howe was waiting to put into operation a similar error; he also was going in the wrong direction.

For many years students of history have studied and puzzled over the events that led to the British movement southward instead of north up the Hudson. General Burgoyne certainly expected the British army to advance to meet him; it was a basic, essential element in his plan. Yet General Howe was never specifically told to make such a move.

The individual responsible for all this confusion was Lord George Germain, the Colonial Secretary, a peculiarly inept individual, who enthusiastically supported Burgoyne's plan, but then failed to send appropriate instructions to General Howe. It would appear that explicit orders were actually prepared for Germain's signature, but then, through carelessness on his part, they were never dispatched. Also, it would appear that Germain did not read, or at least did not understand, Howe's dispatches because that officer never seriously considered going to Burgoyne's aid. The objective upon which he had set his sights was Philadelphia, the capital of the colonies.

It is obvious that the lion's share of the blame for Howe's army going in the wrong direction should be placed squarely upon the shoulders of Lord George Germain because he was the civilian cabinet minister responsible for the coordination of the war in America. However, this fact does not absolve General Howe of all responsibility for having made the wrong decision. He was the senior general officer in North America and therefore responsible, at least indirectly, for the safety of all British troops operating against the American forces. He was a trained soldier, which Germain certainly was not, and furthermore he was in a far better position to judge the probable course of events than Germain, who was 3,000 miles away in London.

General George Washington certainly expected the British in New York to move to the aid of Burgoyne. It was the only logical thing to do if Howe was at all worried about the safety of Burgoyne's army. Over the years a great number of theories have been evolved as to why General Howe left his fellow officer to his fate and chose to go to Philadelphia instead. He has been accused of everything from thoughtlessness, to stupidity, to a desire for personal glory which would outweigh any laurels Burgoyne might attain.

Generations of Americans have been taught that "Billy" Howe was indolent, self-indulgent, and spent far too much of his time with his apparently talented mistress, Mrs. Joshua Loring, and far too little time paying attention to his assigned duties. This description of the enemy general was excellent American wartime propaganda, but there are certain objections to preserving this image of the man. First, to continue to depict the British leader in such an unfavorable light, as an individual possessed of so little merit, is destructive of the reputation of Washington and the other generals who faced

Howe in battle. For, if General Howe was actually such an unworthy opponent, he should have been easily defeated.

Secondly, there must have been some good reason why this man was selected to command the British forces. A hasty examination of General Sir William Howe's career before and during the early part of the American Revolution will provide a ready answer. He was a professional soldier who had joined the British Army at the age of seventeen in time to take part in the War of the Austrian Succession. From that time onward his military service had been continuous, although, like Burgoyne, he had also served as a member of Parliament. During the French and Indian War he had particularly distinguished himself at Quebec. As a major of infantry, Howe personally led twenty-four volunteers up the trail leading to the Plains of Abraham. There he surprised and overpowered the Canadian guard, thus opening the way for Wolfe's decisive victory over Montcalm, which won Canada for England.

At the Battle of Bunker Hill, General Howe gave a remarkable demonstration of leadership and gallantry in action. After the repulse of the second assault, many British officers pleaded with him not to make a third attempt. By then it had become perfectly obvious that the wrong method of attack had been adopted but, even under the stress and strain of battle with British dead and dying on all sides, General Howe was smart enough to realize that the reputation of the British Army in America demanded a third assault, and that the third attack must succeed. At his order, all knapsacks and every superfluous bit of equipment were discarded. Then, trusting in the oft-demonstrated courage of the trained British soldier, he personally, sword in hand, led one of the attack columns against the breastwork on Breed's Hill.

Fourteen months later, General Howe proved beyond the shadow of a doubt that he knew how to fight and win a battle. The result was the victory on Long Island. Why then did this British general who had proved himself a loyal subordinate on many occasions in his service, and was obviously not stupid, fail to go to Burgoyne's aid if he was worried about the latter's safety? The answer, of course, is that it never occurred to him to worry. No British officer in that day and age could visualize such an extraordinary event as a British army being forced to surrender to the American rebels. Furthermore, he had informed Lord Germain of his plans and no objections had been raised to the idea of capturing Philadelphia. Everyone knew that King George was anxious to crush this rebellion quickly. Therefore, let Burgoyne go to Albany while he captured Philadelphia. There was an excellent chance that Washington's army could be destroyed in the process. The American commander-in-chief had fought to save New York from capture; the Americans might also stand and fight to defend their capital city. If the Continental Army could be thoroughly defeated, the war could be brought to a rapid and successful conclusion.

Shortly before setting sail from New York City, a letter came from Burgoyne announcing satisfactory progress at Fort Ticonderoga. In his reply, Howe wrote that he was leaving Sir Henry Clinton in command at New York City to "act as occurrences direct;" then, on July 23, he set sail. While enroute a dispatch came from Germain which showed clearly how confused that individual was. He suggested cooperation with Burgoyne, which by this time was entirely impractical unless Germain, back in London, thought that Howe could actually capture Philadelphia, and then return and help Burgoyne also.

Washington's spies had kept him well informed of the British troop loading. They told him approximately how many soldiers were on board and how many remained in New York, but none could tell him the British destination. For Washington it was the worst sort of guessing game, in which his opponents, the brothers Howe, the admiral and the general, held all the high cards. The British had complete control of the sea. Their warships and transports could simply sail away, and then reappear at any point they chose—at Boston, back at New York, someplace on the road to Philadelphia, or any point farther south. They had complete freedom of maneuver which only control of the sea can give, and Washington could do nothing but wait to see which way to jump.

It was impossible to guard every point. When the fleet sailed, Washington guessed that its destination might be Philadelphia, but he couldn't take a chance that the ships might not come back and sail up the Hudson. Some American troops had already been sent to guard the river. They were not enough to stop Howe's army but they had to remain there; at least they might delay an enemy advance toward the north. With the remainder of his army Washington moved partway toward Philadelphia. The army could not be ordered to march too far to the south because, if Howe did sail back to the Hudson, the American infantry would be left miles behind.

This waiting became extremely nerve-racking, and only one piece of good fortune fell in Washington's lap. An enemy dispatch rider was captured bearing a letter from Howe to Burgoyne announcing Boston as his destination. But the enemy messenger had been captured with such extraordinary ease that this letter could be disregarded: it was obviously a plant, designed to try to deceive. The city of Boston, therefore, was probably not where Howe was going.

Finally, a whole week after the sailing of the fleet, it was sighted off the Capes of the Delaware. Washington moved nearer Philadelphia, and then the fleet sailed out to sea again. The waiting this time was worse than before. If ever in American history the importance of sea power was thoroughly demonstrated, this was one of the most aggravating occasions. Three weeks went by with no news, except from the north where Burgoyne was still apparently making good progress. The American commander-in-chief had already sent some of his best Continental troops to help stop Burgoyne; now he sent Morgan's corps of riflemen. This is a striking illustration of Washington's capacity to think of the difficulties and troubles that others were facing, even though he was at the

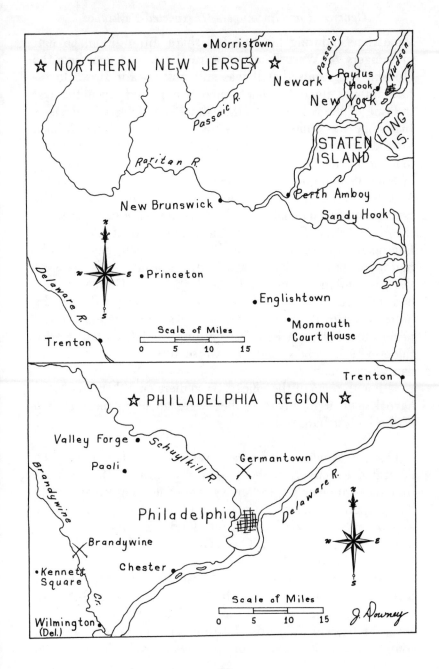

☆ NORTHERN NEW JERSEY ☆

•Morristown

Passaic R.

Newark • •Paulus Hook

New York

Passaic

Hudson

STATEN ISLAND

LONG IS.

Raritan R.

New Brunswick •

•Perth Amboy

Sandy Hook

•Princeton

•Englishtown

•Monmouth Court House

Delaware R.

Trenton •

Scale of Miles

0   5   10   15

Trenton •

☆ PHILADELPHIA REGION ☆

Valley Forge •

Schuylkill R.

Paoli •

×Germantown

Philadelphia

Delaware R.

Brandywine

×Brandywine

Chester

•Kennett Square

Cr.

Wilmington•
(Del.)

Scale of Miles

0   5   10   15

J. Downey

same time enduring his own full share. In addition, he sent messengers to West Point to warn the troops guarding the Hudson Highlands that it was still possible for Howe to return up the river. So much time had passed since the last sighting of the British ships that almost anything was possible. Just as he was about to retrace his own steps and march back toward New York, word came at last that the British fleet was moving up the Chesapeake. For the first time since the month of May, Washington could be certain of his enemy's real plans.

It would be difficult to say whether Washington or the British and Hessian soldiers felt a greater sense of relief when the debarkation finally began near the head of Chesapeake Bay on August 25, 1777. After his long guessing game, Washington was in the right place with his army ready to meet the foe. On the other hand, the British and German troops had been confined in extremely cramped quarters during the hottest days of the year for seven weeks. They were overjoyed to find themselves at long last on firm ground; no battle with the American rebels could be worse torture than what they had already endured.

Although none of the officers or soldiers on either side could have known it in advance, they were about to meet in two of the largest battles of the war.

The ordeal which those men were soon to face cannot be described effectively without some reference to the weapons they took into combat, for any system of fighting is necessarily based upon the arms or armament in use at the time. Today a good rifle can be loaded and fired very rapidly and is accurate at long ranges. The bayonet is seldom used today in hand-to-hand combat.

In the American Revolution almost the exact opposite was true. The standard firearm on both sides was the musket, with a maximum range of only 125 yards, and it was highly inaccurate beyond 75 yards. Loading and firing was a slow, complicated procedure. A bit of powder was placed in the flintlock pan; the remainder of the powder from the paper cartridge was poured into the barrel. With the butt of the piece resting on the ground, a musket ball and some wadding were then rammed down the barrel. When the trigger was pulled there was a long wait. First the powder in the pan had to be ignited by a spark from the flint. Then the flashing of the powder in the pan was supposed to ignite, through a small hole, the powder charge in the chamber. With such a system it is not surprising to learn that the musket misfired almost 10 percent of the time.

A well-trained soldier was supposed to be able to fire three rounds a minute but in the heat of battle, with an enemy charging at him from only 75 yards away, to fire twice before he reached your position would be very good indeed. Armed with such weapons, European armies had developed a system of fighting in lines three men deep. Volley fire, at close range, delivered by three lines of highly trained troops could be terribly effective; accurately aimed fire at individual targets was not necessary.

The standard method of attack was to fire one or two volleys, and then charge with the bayonet to clinch the victory. With such short-range muskets, it was normal for troops to fight hand-to-hand. The bayonet was an all-important weapon; the British regular was superbly trained in its use and had proved his ability on countless European battlefields. Often bayonet charges were made without firing any volleys. Musketry fire at troops behind entrenchments would be almost ineffective anyway. The third assault at Bunker Hill was purely a bayonet charge.

The Americans, on the other hand, confronted, during the French and Indian War, with an enemy who hid behind trees (the Indians never fought in the open) developed a much more widely dispersed method of fighting. Inevitably, when the two systems met, each side began to adopt some of their enemy's tactics. The British began teaching their soldiers to make more use of cover at times and developed light infantry to fight irregular warfare in wooded country; many of the Loyalists who fought for the British were used in this way. The Americans, in order to meet their enemy on open ground, had to teach their most reliable troops to fight in the linear system; if they had not done so they could never have hoped to win on a regular battlefield. However, bayonets were always in short supply. American troops often had to do the best they could without them. Nor were they well trained in their use until General von Steuben taught them how at Valley Forge in 1778.

The legend persists in the United States that all the colonists were trained in the use of firearms from boyhood and were excellent marksmen. It is true that, in its training, the Continental Army paid more attention to aiming at a specific target, but no one could be accurate with the average musket. The legend, of course, has its origin in the rifle used primarily on the western frontier. In New England, for example, the rifle was practically unknown and there was probably not a single rifle used in the Battle of Bunker Hill.

The so-called Kentucky rifle was developed from the hunting rifle used in Switzerland and in the adjacent forests and mountains of Germany. From this basic weapon, American gunsmiths had evolved an extremely accurate firearm of smaller caliber and with a much longer barrel. A real expert could hit a very small target at ranges of 200 yards or more. Unfortunately, it played a secondary role in the war because only a few of these weapons were in existence, and they could not be manufactured in quantity. Also it took about three times as long to load a rifle as a musket. In hand-to-hand combat the weapon was so long as to be unwieldy and, because of the smaller bore, the musket bayonet could not be fitted. Therefore, by far the greater part of the fighting was done by the Continental soldier armed with a short-range musket, not by the expert marksman of American legend. The two battles soon to be fought were excellent examples of this fact.

On September 10, sixteen days after his first troops had landed near the head of Chesapeake Bay, General Howe had concentrated his army at Kennett Square, Pennsylvania. His march to that point had been very slow but he was in no great hurry. The men and horses had needed time to recuperate from their long, confining sea voyage. On the next day he hoped to bring Washington to battle. Washington's American army was in position on the other side of a creek called the Brandywine, apparently ready to stand and fight in defense of Philadelphia. This was exactly what Howe wanted. Some of his officers had insisted that Washington would not dare to make a stand with his new Continental Army still in the process of being trained. It looked as if these advisors were wrong. It was the story of New York City all over again. From a strictly military point of view his enemy should never have attempted to defend New York, but he had been forced to do so by Congress. Now it looked as if Washington was again being forced by public opinion to fight, this time to try to save the colonial capital.

The Loyalists who knew this region had reported that Washington's army was strongly posted at Chadd's Ford, directly across the main road to Philadelphia, The Brandywine itself was not a serious obstacle but the valley was narrow and dominated on each side by steep hills. A frontal attack would be costly, but there was plenty of room to maneuver. It was fairly open country, reasonably suitable for the type of warfare in which his men were better trained than the enemy. And, most important of all, it would appear that the Americans had neglected to guard the upper fords in strength. Furthermore, Howe had been told that passable roads existed by which he could move around, cross the creek, and envelop the American right flank. If it worked it would be the Battle of Long Island all over again, except that the army would be hitting the enemy's right instead of the left flank.

At Long Island General Howe had taken about half his army on the march around the enemy. This time he decided to go with two-thirds of his entire force, leaving one-third to make a demonstration to hold Washington's attention. To be in charge of the holding attack he selected Lieutenant General Wilhelm von Knyphausen, his trusted German leader who had served so well at the capture of Fort Washington the preceding November. For this part of his scheme, Howe allotted von Knyphausen a total of 5,000 men, including some British troops and an abnormal amount of artillery. Howe gave very careful instructions to his subordinate. The mission was to march to Chadd's Ford and there make a demonstration which would lead his enemies to believe that the entire army was present and about to attack across the creek. The inclusion of British troops and the unusual amount of artillery should help to convince Washington that the whole army was facing him. The longer this illusion could be maintained, the greater chance of success the flank attack would have.

The main effort, then, would be made around the American right flank. Major General Lord Charles Cornwallis was placed in command of this force of 10,000 men, which included some German jägers armed with short, heavy, large rifles of limited range. General Howe chose to march with this column.

About 4:00 A.M., on September 11, Howe, Cornwallis, and the 10,000 troops began their march from Kennett Square. After a little more than two miles had been covered, the column turned abruptly to its left and disappeared northward. About 9:30, von Knyphausen's 5,000 troops, following behind the main body but keeping straight toward Chadd's Ford, ran into strong resistance. Gradually, the Americans, occupying successive delaying positions, were driven back across the ford to the other side of the Brandywine. The Germans and British occupied the high ground west of the creek and made preparations as if for an assault. They opened with cannon fire upon the American positions, and kept it up all the rest of the morning and into the afternoon, wondering how much time would pass before they would hear the sound of other guns, announcing the arrival of Cornwallis on the enemy flank.

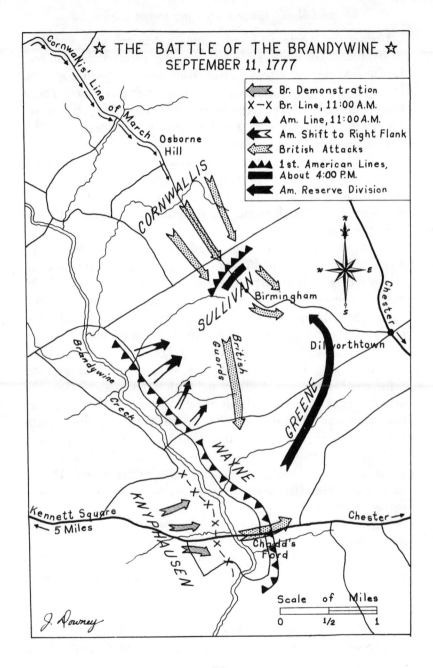

☆ THE BATTLE OF THE BRANDYWINE ☆
SEPTEMBER 11, 1777

	Br. Demonstration
X—X	Br. Line, 11:00 A.M.
▲▲	Am. Line, 11:00 A.M.
	Am. Shift to Right Flank
	British Attacks
▬▬	1st. American Lines, About 4:00 P.M.
	Am. Reserve Division

Cornwallis' Line of March

Osborne Hill

CORNWALLIS

SULLIVAN

Birmingham

Chester

Dilworthtown

Brandywine Creek

British Guards

GREENE

WAYNE

KNYPHAUSEN

Kennett Square
← 5 Miles

Chester →

Chadd's Ford

J. Downey

Scale of Miles

0   1/2   1

Cornwallis' troops had had a long, hot march over winding, dusty roads but apparently no one had spotted the column. In the distance, at intervals, von Knyphausen's guns could be heard, and those of the Americans returning the fire. There had been no sudden increase in the cannonade; therefore, everything presumably was going according to plan. Brandy-wine Creek had been crossed and was behind them. It was now 2:30 P.M.—would it not be advisable to take time out for rest and food before advancing to the attack? Since the enemy had given no indication that their flank movement had been discovered, Cornwallis and Howe halted the 10,000 men on Osborne Hill.

By 3:30, the British were ready to advance. The troops were formed in three divisions. On the right of the line, in the place of honor, were the British Guards; in the middle were the grenadiers; on their left were the light infantry and the jägers. About 4:00 P.M., the order was given; the advance began and the men moved forward as steadily and calmly as if on parade, with the bands playing "The British Grenadier."

About a mile to the front the Americans were hastily going into position. As the artillery on both sides opened fire, the attack struck. The brigade at the right end of the American line gave way in confusion. The British Guards collided with the brigade at the left of the American line just as it was coming into position, trying to form on the field. This last brigade had no chance of making an effective stand. It had been caught at the worst possible moment, and it also was driven backward.

Thus, at the very beginning of the battle, both ends of the American right wing had been forced to give way. An easy success seemed assured, but then the attacking troops, after plunging forward only a very short distance, were brought to a sudden halt in front of a new defensive line.

Outnumbered nearly three to one, the remaining Americans held fast their new line, and repulsed the attack. This was a little difficult for the British generals to understand. They organized another assault. The Americans now were forced to retreat, but here they came surging forward again. Five times the defenders were driven from their position; each time they counterattacked and regained the line. Officers who had been in many a battle in Europe could not recall having seen any troops fight more bravely than these. Finally they withdrew, but only after their officers ordered them to go. The flank attack had been held up for nearly two hours, but soldiers, generally without bayonets, could not be expected to hold forever.

Cornwallis' men sprang forward to pursue. During that tough two-hour battle they had acquired a tremendously increased respect for their opponents, but now was the time to reap the rewards of their victory. They gained less than a mile before they ran headlong into another American division, which opened ranks to let its comrades through, then closed again to stop the pursuers in their tracks. Here again the fighting was bitter and prolonged, with frequent bayonet charges. So close were the battle lines that the Anspach jägers recognized Brigadier General Muhlenberg, the gallant Lutheran pastor who had served as a soldier in Germany in his youth. They hailed him with delight: *"Hier kommt Teufel Piet."*

General Howe, directing the battle, could not have been too surprised at the appearance of the other American division. Obviously, they had come from the forces opposing von Knyphausen at Chadd's Ford. Now, if only that veteran officer was performing the task assigned to him, all would work out well, as planned.

As a matter of fact, General von Knyphausen had proved to be exactly the right man for the job assigned. All day, until hearing Cornwallis' guns, he had kept the Americans at Chadd's Ford occupied. When the sounds of battle reached him, his troops were formed and, with perfect timing, his assault was launched across the ford just as some of the troops opposing him were leaving to confront Cornwallis on the other flank. The Americans at the ford resisted valiantly until suddenly they were struck in the right and rear by the British Guards who, after the defeat of the first American defense line on the right wing, had plunged straight ahead through the woods instead of becoming involved in the rest of the battle. This finished all American hopes for a successful defense at Chadd's Ford.

Now, on both wings, the defenders were fighting to save themselves by holding, if possible, until darkness would cover their retreat. On both flanks, to General Howe's surprise, they managed to accomplish this feat. During the night they streamed back along the road to Chester, protected by rear guards moving in good order.

The British plan had worked to perfection, but it was extraordinary how well the Americans had faced the ordeal, like veterans. As it happened, the American forces on the battlefield had numbered 11,000 against the British 15,000. About 1,000 of these had been militia but Washington had wisely placed them about a mile and half downstream below Chadd's Ford where there was little chance of a crossing being attempted. They had taken practically no part in the battle. Almost all the rest of the 10,000 Americans who had given such an excellent account of themselves had been Continental soldiers, most of them from Virginia and Pennsylvania.

Now General Howe and the entire British and Hessian army looked confidently forward to the successful capture of Philadelphia. The Battle of the Brandywine had been more costly than they expected. British and German losses in killed, wounded, and missing had been close to 600 men. Naturally they assumed that the Americans had suffered greater casualties; the loser in a battle of this sort almost always does. Howe's estimate was 900 killed and wounded plus 400 prisoners, a total of 1,300. The actual count has never been accurately determined but 1,000 casualties would be a better guess, which amounts to 10 percent of the soldiers actually engaged.

After allowing his army time to rest and reorganize, General Howe sent his men forward again. He felt sure there would be no further large engagements in the immediate future. The American forces, after their defeat and a 10 percent loss in personnel, would be unable to fight another large-scale battle. Philadelphia was now his for the taking. Nine days later there occurred an event which confirmed his impressions. On the night of September 20, Major General Charles Grey completely surprised General Anthony Wayne's men encamped near Paoli. The attack was executed under cover of darkness with the bayonet only; all muskets had their flints knocked out so there would be no chance of a shot being fired even by accident. As a result the British general was thereafter known as "No-flint" Grey. The action has gone down in history as the "Paoli Massacre," but there is no justification for such a name. It was a superbly planned and efficiently executed night assault. The American loss may have been as high as 300 casualties; General Grey lost less than 10 killed and wounded. That the affair became known as a massacre was mainly the result of good American propaganda designed to make Wayne's soldiers eager to take revenge. On September 26, two weeks and one day after the Battle of the Brandywine, which had made its capture practically certain, the British marched into Philadelphia.

If, six days after the seizure of the colonial capital, General Howe had been permitted to attend a council of war at Washington's headquarters he would have been greatly amazed. The leaders of the defeated army were actually planning a dawn attack on the victors. The defeat at the Brandywine had not depressed the men who had fought there nearly as much as the British had supposed. The American troops felt, and rightly so, that they had given a good account of themselves. The Continental Army, formed so hastily from recruits and more experienced soldiers with a year's service, had, with four months training, done surprisingly well. The soldiers were ready and eager to come back and try again another day.

At the same time Washington and his general officers were

also willing to make another effort. They knew full well what had gone wrong back there at Chadd's Ford. They had been completely deceived by Howe's maneuvers, and by conflicting reports received during that day which they had not analyzed correctly. Secretly, to themselves, they may have admitted the well-known axiom that it takes far longer to train an officer to do his part on a battlefield than it does to train the soldiers. The officers of the British army facing them were better trained and had more experience, but if a good chance came and conditions looked favorable they would try again.

On the evening of October 2, conditions did look favorable. The British were having trouble maintaining their line of supplies stretching back from Philadelphia to Chesapeake Bay. A total of 3,000 men had been detached from the main army to guard this supply line against raids by the local militia. To open up a shorter route for ships to bring supplies direct to the city, Admiral Howe was presently engaged in trying to batter his way up the Delaware River, which was guarded by American fortifications. Troops from the British forces in Philadelphia had been detached to help in this endeavor. The major part of the British army was now encamped near the little village of Germantown, six miles north of the city. Cornwallis had been left in command at Philadelphia. As a result of all these detachments, Howe had only about 9,000 men with him.

Some Continental reinforcements had arrived to take the place of those lost at the Brandywine. There were also about 3,000 militia available. Washington and his officers decided to take advantage of the situation. In doing so they showed both good judgment and lack of experience. There were to be four attacking columns, marching sixteen miles or more over different roads, to arrive simultaneously at 5:00 A.M. and make a predawn assault together. The two center columns, due to deliver the main attack, were to be composed almost exclusively of Continental troops. The two flanking columns, which were to assist, were to be made up of militia. That part of the plan showed good judgment; it was far safer to depend for the main assault on the better trained, more reliable soldiers.

On the other hand, experience with troops on maneuvers would have taught the American leaders that such a plan as they had devised was far too complicated. A night march over varying distances with no means of communication between the columns almost certainly would not work as planned. One column would be sure to arrive ahead of the others; some might not arrive at all. As it happened, the column which had been given too great a distance to march to the objective was one of the militia columns. It arrived too late to take part in the action. The other militia column contented itself with doing a little bit of firing at the enemy from a distance. As far as the British who took part in the coming battle were concerned, the attack upon them was made only by the Continental troops in the two center columns.

Five o'clock in the morning had been too early an hour to set for completion of a night march of so many miles over such winding country roads. On October 4, 1777, about six o'clock on a very foggy morning, as the sun was just coming up, the first of the two American center columns struck a British picket near Mount Airy on the Skippack Road. It was not the complete surprise that Washington's night march to Trenton had achieved. British patrols had already discovered that an American force of some sort was approaching. Most of the British pickets had already received a warning to be on the alert. General Howe had been notified, but he and his staff officers had assumed that the Americans constituted only a small reconnaissance party. After all, the defeated Americans were still licking the wounds they had received at the Brandywine.

The Mount Airy picket was quickly driven back, but not before it had fired two signal guns to alert the British forces. The infantry regiment on outpost duty in that area formed quickly and attacked the leading American brigade, stopping it in its tracks. The whole American column had to deploy in order to

73

continue the advance. Colonel Thomas Musgrave, the officer in command of that British regiment, the 40th Foot, retreated slowly, firing and then falling back. He was buying time for the army, time it needed to prepare for the coming battle.

By now it should have been clear that this was no mere reconnaissance, but at this moment, General Howe rode onto the battlefield. Unable to believe that the American army could bounce back so vigorously after their defeat, he shouted, "I never saw you retreat before! It's only a scouting party!" To the delight of his men, a volley of grapeshot smashed through the trees over his head. There was his answer. A real battle was under way. Howe galloped back to form his army to meet the attack.

The fog that morning, instead of dissipating, had grown thicker, so dense in fact that a man could not see more than 30 to 40 yards. Covered by the thick fog, Colonel Musgrave was able to move his regiment into the Chew House. It was a fine, large stone building standing well back from the road, the property of Benjamin Chew, former Chief Justice of Pennsylvania. The 40th Foot closed the thick shutters and barricaded the doors. Colonel Musgrave had found a splendid fort with a large lawn giving him an excellent field of fire. Before the end of the battle General Howe would have cause to be thankful that Colonel Musgrave held that position.

The leading Americans streamed past the Chew House to strike the main British line of resistance, which, hurriedly formed in front of their camp, was awaiting attack.

About this time the second American column was driving in the outposts on the right of the British line. There was no way in the world for anyone on either side to gauge accurately what would happen next. The fog was so thick, and the sounds of battle were so distorted by it, that intelligent, coordinated action or the exercise of command of more than a regiment was practically impossible. It was almost every unit for itself. The defending British and Germans could only guess where the attackers might strike. Coordination of the attacking columns

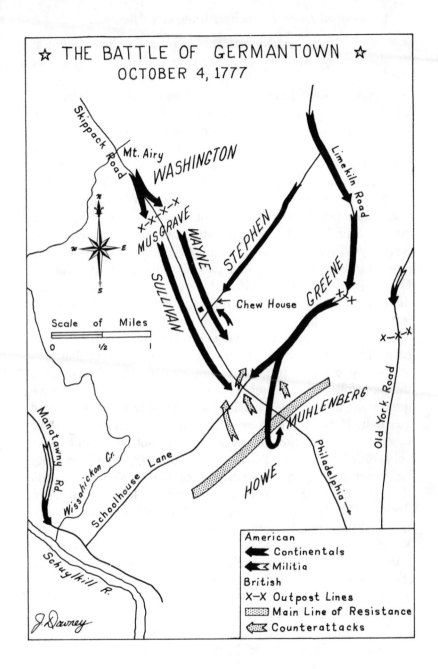

☆ THE BATTLE OF GERMANTOWN ☆
OCTOBER 4, 1777

American
Continentals
Militia
British
X—X Outpost Lines
Main Line of Resistance
Counterattacks

Scale of Miles

J. Davney

75

was out of the question, yet they struck the British almost simultaneously, near the right end, and about the center of the line.

From this point onward, a description of the battle from the British-German viewpoint would not give a clear picture of what happened. In the all-encompassing fog the defending army could not see what really took place. In fact, the Americans never had a very clear idea of what happened until afterward when the reports could be pieced together.

The first American column, with which Washington rode, was under the command of Major General John Sullivan. It consisted of Sullivan's own division and one commanded by Anthony Wayne. Behind it marched the army reserve composed of another division and two brigades. After passing the Chew House, Sullivan had continued straight ahead with his division on the right of the Skippack Road and Wayne's on the left.

Sullivan's decision to leave the Chew House to be taken care of at a later date by the troops following behind was aboslutely correct. It is most unfortunate that Washington did not follow his example. The army reserve should have gone right around the building, leaving only a small force to guard it. If the battle were won, the Chew House could be taken care of at the army's leisure; if not, it would make very little difference. Washington, however, consulted with his generals and, upon the advice of Henry Knox, who said that an enemy strongpoint should not be left in your rear, decided that it must be reduced before the army could continue its advance in safety. The place was surrounded and Knox's artillery was turned upon it. The front door was smashed by the common balls; so were the windows and all the beautiful statuary in the yard, but the artillery had no effect whatever upon the thick stone walls. Efforts to set it afire also failed.

Meanwhile, the second of the American columns, commanded by Major General Nathanael Greene, and consisting of more than half the army, had emerged upon the scene. Their route had been a longer one and, also, their guide had lost his way in the darkness. Greene's men drove through the outposts on the right of the enemy line and advanced to the attack concurrently with Sullivan's and Wayne's troops.

But one of Greene's divisions, commanded by Major General Adam Stephen, had disappeared into the fog. Hearing the roar of cannon around the Chew House, Stephen had turned aside and, without orders, marched his division to render aid at that place. This lone house, with one British regiment, had thus attracted the attention of a tremendous part of the American army. There was more yet to come.

When Greene and Sullivan, with his troops and those of Wayne, launched their attacks, the moral effect was much greater than the effect the same number of men would have produced on a clear day. The British and Hessians, because of the fog, could not see how many troops were involved. One of Greene's brigades, that of Muhlenberg, actually broke through into the rear of the enemy's position, causing a great amount of confusion.

At this moment the sound of firing around the Chew House redoubled in volume. Stephen's artillery had added its thunder to Knox's guns. Anthony Wayne, having no communication with Sullivan on his right, thought that Sullivan was in trouble back there; he swung back to help him. Seeing Wayne's men approaching in the fog from the direction of the British line, Stephen's troops mistook them for the enemy and fired upon them, starting a small battle between themselves.

When Wayne left the front, of course the pressure of Sullivan's attack lessened, and his men were running low on ammunition. Alert British officers seized the opportunity and launched vigorous counterattacks upon both flanks of Sullivan's division. Attacked on both sides, with the sound of fighting around the Chew House increasing in volume to their rear, the Americans of Sullivan's division retired hastily.

This left Greene to face the enemy alone. The British who

had just driven Sullivan from the field turned upon Greene's flank. Those to his front also launched a counterattack. Ignoring the superior numbers about to overwhelm him, Greene held his position to give Muhlenberg a fighting chance to extricate his brigade which had penetrated over a thousand yards behind the enemy line. Gallant Peter Muhlenberg swung about, 180 degrees change of front, and charged back the way he had come. By his swift, vigorous action, he saved most of his men. General Greene then withdrew, thus ending the Battle of Germantown.

Regardless of the claims of some historians, Howe's army had not been very close to defeat at Germantown. Plans had been made to withdraw in case of necessity, but these were only normal precautionary measures that any intelligent commander would take. The line had been pierced at one point but British infantry do not give way or frighten easily; they have a worldwide, justly deserved reputation for being very stubborn in defense of a position.

About 9,000 men on each side took part in this battle and, as at Brandywine, the Americans were almost all from the Continental Army. The defending British and Hessians lost over 500 killed, wounded, and captured, while the attackers suffered casualties totaling over 1,000 killed, wounded, and missing.

The surrender at Saratoga, which occurred shortly thereafter, has taken the spotlight of history away from Germantown; consequently, this battle has not received the attention it deserves. The American public was depressed by yet another defeat following so rapidly upon the heels of the capture of their capital at Philadelphia, but they had no cause to be. Their army had greatly surprised all interested foreign observers. The experienced, knowledgeable generals and statesmen of Europe, who previously had thought of the American patriots as a sort of disorganized rabble, were impressed beyond measure when they heard that the Continental Army had counterattacked at Germantown, so soon after its defeat at the Brandywine, and had given such a splendid account of itself.

Of course, these men observing the conflict from afar had no way of knowing exactly what had actually occurred. Nor did they care particularly whether the British-Hessian army had been close to defeat. When the news of Saratoga reached the French Government, the name Germantown helped influence its decision.

As for General Howe, that officer changed his outlook a bit in several respects. His efforts of the previous year to bring about a reconciliation had failed. There was obviously a hard core of patriots who would have to be thoroughly defeated before they would again submit to British rule. The capture of their capital had in no way affected their resolution to continue the struggle. This was not too surprising; he had not expected the rebellion to collapse simply because he captured Philadelphia. But apparently the Battle of the Brandywine had not inflicted as much injury upon the Americans as he had imagined. The battle had gained Philadelphia, but these Continentals had bounced back too fast. Reluctantly he came to the conclusion that he still had an army capable of offensive action facing him. Under his command the British and Hessians had won victories but the war was obviously far from being won. To avoid future occurrences similar to Germantown, Howe ordered fortifications built to guard the approaches to Philadelphia. At this time it may have occurred to him to wonder if perhaps he had not given the patriots too much time to collect and train an army, or even whether it might not have been wiser to have cooperated with Burgoyne on the Hudson.

4

Benedict Arnold's Heroic Days

Benedict Arnold will always be the most controversial figure of the American Revolution. For years it was the general practice simply to denounce him bitterly for turning traitor. Then a number of writers at least began to explain Arnold's reasons for deserting the cause for which he had fought so brilliantly. There will be no attempt here to add to the wealth of literature on this subject.

Benedict Arnold has already appeared on several occasions in this narrative. His contributions to the success of the patriot cause during the year 1775 through 1777 were many and varied. Together with Ethan Allen he captured Ticonderoga in May, 1775. Later in the same year Arnold led the tortuous expedition through the wilderness northward to Quebec. After the unsuccessful attempt to storm that fortress, though suffering acutely from a wound sustained in the assault, he stayed there to prolong the hopeless effort throughout the winter. Though further injured by a fall from his horse, which forced him to relinquish command at Quebec, he performed yeoman service on the retreat from Canada in the spring of 1776. All through the succeeding summer Benedict Arnold inspired and supervised construction of the American fleet on Lake Champlain, and then took it out to fight the larger British fleet at Valcour Island. As previously recorded, his delaying action during this year on Lake Champlain may well have saved the Revolution.

Even when not on active duty with the army, opportunities for battle appeared on Arnold's doorstep. In April, 1777, a raiding party from New York City invaded his native state of Connecticut to burn stores at Danbury. Arnold so distinguished himself in this action that the Congress finally promoted him to major general, a rank they should have given him much earlier. Washington then sent him northward to join the forces assembling to oppose Burgoyne.

Actually two major generals were sent. The other was Benjamin Lincoln of Massachusetts. It should be noted that both were from New England, because this was intentional on Washington's part. The commander-in-chief was well aware of the fact that the department commander, Major General Philip Schuyler, was disliked and distrusted by the people of New England. Washington hoped that the militia would turn out more readily if they knew that both of Schuyler's principal assistants were from New England.

Both Arnold and Lincoln worked well under Schuyler. They respected and trusted him. Neither joined in the quarrels that continually arose between the pro-Schuyler (New York) party and the anti-Schuyler (New England) faction. A striking example of Arnold's loyalty to his New York chief occurred in the final days of Schuyler's tenure of command.

Fort Stanwix was under siege by St. Leger. General Nicholas Herkimer had organized an expedition to attempt the relief of the garrison but had been stopped at the Battle of Oriskany. News of that viciously fought battle had just been received at Schuyler's headquarters. He called a council of war and proposed that troops be sent to relieve Fort Stanwix, which was still under siege and surely could not hold much longer. The New England faction objected violently because sending an expedition into the Mohawk Valley would weaken the forces opposed to Burgoyne. This argument would have made good sense only if there were any prospect of a large-scale battle being fought against Burgoyne's army in the near future. Everyone present knew that, if Burgoyne chose to advance at that moment, the Americans would have to retreat again, whether troops were sent to relieve Fort Stanwix or not.

However, additional Continental units were on the way, sent by Washington. By the time these arrived, the Stanwix relief expedition would surely have returned. Then, and then only, could the Americans hope to face the British and Hessians in battle.

In that council of war it was quite obvious that the New England faction was objecting to Schuyler's proposal on general principles, simply because Schuyler himself had offered it. Living as we do today in a united country, it is difficult to realize how much people of that era distrusted the residents of other states. To understand their feelings toward each other we must first remind ourselves that the people of the thirteen colonies were composed of many diverse elements: Puritans and Cavaliers, Pilgrims and Catholics, Quakers and French Huguenots, Dutch and Swedish, to name a few. Communication between colonies was difficult. There was little opportunity for the inhabitants of one section to learn to know and understand those in another.

One of the toughest problems facing the leaders of the struggling new country was getting the various states to cooperate with each other. The southerners from Maryland, Virginia, the Carolinas, and Georgia were suspicious of those who lived in the Middle Atlantic states and were distrustful of the straitlaced Yankees. The New Englanders returned these feelings with interest and, in addition, there was a special reason why they were particularly cautious in dealing with New Yorkers. For years both New Hampshire and New York had claimed the land which is now the state of Vermont. During the Revolution this territory was commonly called the New Hampshire Grants because most of the people who had settled there had done so as a result of grants of land received from the Governor of New Hampshire. Both states claimed jurisdiction, but the more numerous settlers from New England had defied New York's claims, and a considerable amount of blood had been shed as a result. Relations between these two sections were therefore particularly strained. Usually all anyone had to do to get a good fight started was to call a New Yorker a "damn Yankee."

In General Schuyler's council of war there were many present who knew of rumors being spread that Schuyler had turned traitor, that Fort Ticonderoga had been sold to the British. There was a fantastic tale circulating in the camp that Burgoyne had bought the fort by firing bullets of silver to be presented to Schuyler as part of the purchase price.

In this atmosphere of distrust, it was Benedict Arnold who sprang to the defense of his commander who was being accused of treachery. When General Schuyler, angered by the objections being raised by some of his subordinates, announced that he would take full responsibility for the decision to save Fort Stanwix, the first to volunteer for the task was Arnold. It is an odd fact of history that Benedict Arnold was the New Englander who felt so confident of his combat record in the war that he never for a second hesitated to ally himself with the general whom some of his compatriots were accusing of treason.

The manner in which Arnold successfully completed his assigned mission has already been described. It took only a few days, but when he returned with his troops, a new general had arrived to take the command of the army away from Philip Schuyler.

For many months Major General Horatio Gates had been scheming to have the Continental Congress appoint him in place of Schuyler. He had found favor with the New England delegates who were clamoring for Schuyler's removal. After endless discussion and much acrimonious debate, enough votes were found to have Gates elected.

Now at the time General Arnold volunteered to lead Schuyler's proposed expedition against St. Leger he must have known, or at least heard rumors, that Schuyler was about to be relieved from command. (As a matter of fact the Congress had already voted, but the news had probably not yet reached the conferees at the council of war.) Benedict Arnold's ready offer to carry out Schuyler's plans was not the act of a good politician. Arnold had never been a good politician. He was tactless, impatient, extremely outspoken, and had made numerous enemies unnecessarily. Thus when Gates appeared, with Arnold absent, all of Arnold's enemies were on hand to give the new commander their version of what had happened at the council of war. As the campaign progressed, the ill feeling between the two senior generals intensified. It did not help matters any that General Gates had an aide, a major named James Wilkinson, who did his best to feed the flames of animosity in hopes that he himself might profit thereby.

Just before the return of the Fort Stanwix relief expedition, Colonel Daniel Morgan arrived in the American camp with his Continental Army corps of expert riflemen; to this unit Gates promptly attached 250 selected Continental light infantrymen under the command of Major Henry Dearborn, who had served with Arnold and Morgan on the march to Quebec. With these and other Continental Army units sent by Washington, and with the return early in September of Arnold's expedition, General Gates was in a position that his predecessor, Schuyler, had never been able to attain. For the first time since the beginning of the campaign, the Americans outnumbered the invading army. Almost all the Indians had left Burgoyne. Only a few British reinforcements had been received, not nearly enough to replace all the troop losses. The invading army had only about 6,000 men fit for duty. The Americans, on the other hand, could count 7,000, and a large portion of these were regular Continentals.

By early September it had become perfectly obvious to both sides that Burgoyne would have to move one way or the other, either forward or backward, very shortly. There was every indication that he planned to move forward. After the Battle of Bennington, the British-German army had been halted to bring up supplies. Certainly this would not have been done if the invaders planned to retreat. Burgoyne was still on the east side of the river; he would have to cross to the west side in order to reach Albany. Expecting that this crossing would probably be made soon, Gates sent Morgan and his riflemen forward to scout the enemy's movements. To prepare to meet the British advance, the American army, on September 12, occupied a strong position on a high bluff named Bemis Heights, just north of the town of Stillwater, and began preparing breastworks and trenches.

On the next day, September 13, Burgoyne's army began crossing the Hudson River on a bridge of boats. The crossing was made at Saratoga, which has since been renamed Schuylerville. By September 15, all British and German troops were on the west shore. The southward movement then began in a slow, methodical manner. With the loss of most of the Indians, the advancing army was, in a military sense, moving blind. The Indians had been no help at all in battles like Hubbardton or Bennington, but they had been fairly useful as scouts. Now, with Morgan's men roaming the woods, the few Indians remaining with Burgoyne were very cautious. As a result, General Gates was kept fully informed of his enemy's movements. On September 18, the American commanders knew that the enemy had halted some three miles north of their position and were making preparations for an attack, which might be launched on the morrow.

The American position on Bemis Heights was well chosen and the defenses had been carefully laid out by the Polish engineer Thaddeus Kosciusko. First, there were some trenches and breastworks near the riverbank, stretching across the main road. Then, from near the water's edge, a high bluff rose steeply. On the top of this bluff, which towered from 100 to 200 feet above the river, the main defensive position was laid out. It formed three sides of an irregular square, with the rear side left open. To the front there was a ravine, and on the left (west) side there was another ravine. The troops had labored on these positions for six days, digging firing trenches protected by log and earth embankments, providing gun emplacements, and even erecting small redoubts. The position was very strong and would have been extremely difficult to carry by assault. But there was another hill, about 100 feet higher, across the shallow ravine on the west side, which had not been fortified. If an enemy should occupy this position and emplace artillery there, his guns could fire just as effectively upon the American positions as the American guns could play upon any British troops attacking from the front or along the riverbank.

On the morning of September 19, American scouts reported an unusual amount of activity in the enemy camp. There were definite indications that something out of the ordinary was afoot. About 10:00 A.M., three columns marched out toward the American lines. One moved by the river road; a second column advanced along a road through the forest about a mile inland. The third and largest column marched westward; its mission was to get beyond the American left flank before turning southward. Perched in treetops and roving the woods beside the columns, the American scouts were able to keep fairly close tabs on the enemy and send back reports to General Gates.

All during the morning intelligence of the enemy movements flowed in to Gates' headquarters, but no action resulted. He seemed quite content to gather the information, sift the reports, and await the attack in his prepared positions. All during the morning General Arnold, who commanded the troops on the American left wing, fretted, fumed, and pleaded with General Gates to send troops forward to engage the advancing British and Hessians before they reached Bemis Heights.

The two American generals were in complete disagreement as to the proper course to pursue. Horatio Gates had been keeping his men hard at work for the last six days to prepare a strong defensive position. Extensive fortifications had been built for the sole purpose of stopping the British advance at Bemis Heights. Why should he, then, as soon as the enemy made an appearance, abandon the result of all this effort and rush forward into the woods to the front of the position? To Gates' way of thinking it seemed much more intelligent to stay where he was, and follow out the original plan of forcing the enemy to make an assault upon the Americans in their prepared fortifications.

Benedict Arnold was of the exact opposite opinion. By nature he was impetuous, aggressive, alert, and eager for battle under almost any circumstances. But it was more than just a simple desire for action that caused him now to urge Gates to sally forth to meet the enemy. In the course of the last two years of warfare, Arnold had been under fire on numerous occasions. He was thoroughly acquainted with the tactical methods of the British and Hessians. He knew full well that the enemy was better trained than the Americans for fighting in open fields and fairly level country, but that the Americans were superior when it came to fighting in woods and forests. At this very moment the enemy army was preparing for an advance over some two miles of country superbly suited to the American style of combat—tall trees and thick woods, with only a few small clearings. Furthermore, close at hand and ready for action, was the best group of soldiers trained for this type of combat in the world—Colonel Daniel Morgan's Pennsylvania, Maryland, and Virginia backwoodsmen, ably supported by Lieutenant Colonel Henry Dearborn's light infantry.

Finally, about noon, General Gates agreed to send Morgan's Continentals out in front of the left wing toward the strongest enemy column. Shortly afterward, about 1:00 P.M., three guns were fired by the British. This was the signal for their three columns to advance.

Morgan's men soon discovered a group of the enemy in a ravine south of Freeman's Farm, a clearing covering about fifteen acres, from which the battle takes its name. Taking careful aim, the riflemen fired. As officers and men fell, the enemy fled. Morgan's riflemen poured across the clearing,

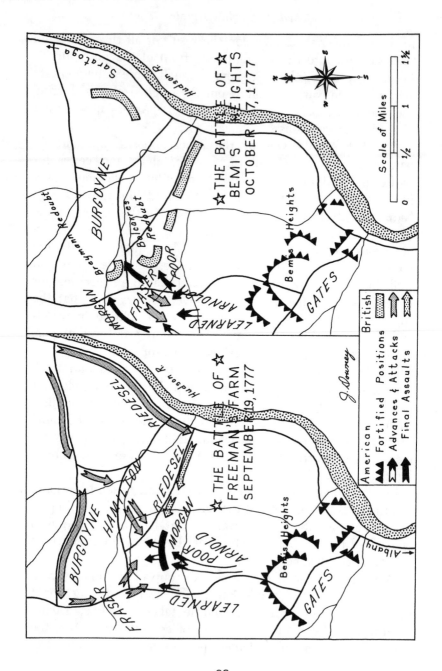

THE BATTLE OF BEMIS HEIGHTS
OCTOBER 7, 1777

THE BATTLE OF FREEMAN'S FARM
SEPTEMBER 19, 1777

Scale of Miles

American
Fortified Positions
Advances & Attacks
Final Assaults

British

J. Downey

but victory was not to be that simple. A volley rang out; a strong enemy line appeared, to drive the attackers back into the woods. Hastily, to rally his dispersed troops, Colonel Morgan sounded his turkey call; the scattered soldiers responded and the battle began in earnest. Two regiments of New Hampshire Continentals, sent by Arnold, appeared on the scene. Additional enemy troops arrived; artillery opened fire. General Arnold assumed command, bringing into the battle the remainder of General Enoch Poor's New Hampshire and New York brigade, with two regiments of Connecticut militia attached. Here on the battlefield was developed an excellent method of utilizing comparatively untrained militia. Aligned with dependable troops of the Continental Army, trusting in the disciplined courage of these steady, reliable units whom they knew would not panic, inspired by the leadership of a fighting officer like Arnold, a man from their own state, the militia stood and fought exceedingly well.

With the sure instinct of a born combat leader, Arnold grasped the fact that he was directly opposite the point where the right and center columns of the enemy came together. This was bound to be a weak spot where control by officers of the opposing army would be least effective. He concentrated the American efforts there to break through. Time and again Arnold led his men forward across the clearing; time and again the Americans were driven back by resolute bayonet charges. But the enemy line was bending inward under the pressure of the assaults. In this type of terrain, in this type of fighting, the British were suffering greater casualties, including many at the hands of the expert American riflemen. Losses among the officers and the artillery gun crews were especially heavy. Arnold felt sure he could break the line. If only Gates would send reinforcements. But that gentleman consistently refused until late in the afternoon, when he sent General Ebenezer Learned's brigade of Massachusetts and New York Continentals. Through some error this brigade appeared at the left end of the American line, attacking the right flank of the far right British column. Before this mistake could be corrected, the situation was dramatically and radically altered.

The commander of the German division of Burgoyne's army was Major General Baron Friedrich Adolf von Riedesel, an experienced, thoroughly capable, highly intelligent officer who had served in the armies of Germany for over twenty years. Throughout the campaign he had proved a tower of strength; at Hubbardton, for example, when the result of that battle seemed in doubt, it was von Riedesel who had turned the tide.

His family had also contributed. The vivacious, young, and pretty Baroness had insisted on accompanying him, with their three very small daughters. Their presence had gone far toward making life more pleasant and endurable in this strange North American wilderness not only for the Baron but for many of his friends in the German and British contingents, some of whom had also brought their wives with them.

In the Battle of Freeman's Farm, General von Riedesel was in command of the left column, the one closest to the river. As yet, his men had been only lightly engaged. Hearing the gunfire, Major General William Phillips, Burgoyne's second-in-command, who had been marching with von Riedesel, hastily departed to lend a hand to Burgoyne who was with the hard-pressed center column. Phillips had sent back for more artillery; then nothing more had been heard from him although the clamor of battle grew steadily in volume. Von Riedesel was not like Gates; he could not sit idly by, listening to the battle rage close by him and do nothing. On his own initiative, the German commander stopped the march of his column, swiftly formed a reinforced regiment, and led it personally to the sound of the guns. His sudden attack, bursting upon the American right flank, changed the fortunes of the day.

The American hero of the battle, Benedict Arnold, with 3,000 men (Morgan's and Dearborn's Continentals, Poor's brigade with its attached militia, plus Learned's brigade, which came in late) had almost won Freeman's Farm. General Gates had sat in his tent, with 4,000 men standing by, just listening to the sounds of the battle. Of the 3,000 actually engaged, the Americans lost over 10 percent, over 300 killed, wounded, and missing.

General Burgoyne had done little better than Gates. With 6,000 effectives, he had sent only 4,200 men into the attack, leaving 1,800 as a reserve which he never used. The center column had borne the brunt of the battle throughout the day. One British regiment in this column, the 62nd Foot, had stood its ground taking 80 percent casualties. Perhaps 3,000 British and Germans had fought and their losses had amounted to about 600 killed, wounded, and captured, 20 percent of the total number engaged. These figures prove that General Arnold was absolutely correct in his contention that Americans would have the upper hand, with their tactical methods, in this type of terrain. From this battle, von Riedesel emerged as the hero of the winning side.

General Arnold, on the other hand, to his complete amazement, was not even mentioned by Gates in his report of the battle to the Continental Congress. Now, if there was one sure way to irritate Benedict Arnold, it was to fail to give him recognition for things he had achieved. A bitter quarrel resulted in Gates relieving Arnold of his command, but, fortunately, the latter did not leave the camp, as he threatened. It was apparent that another battle would soon be fought and, with or without a command, Arnold was not the man to miss a chance to distinguish himself. This is in sharp contrast to the actions of General John Stark and his men who had fought and won the Battle of Bennington. With great difficulty, Benjamin Lincoln had persuaded them to come join the American army. They had arrived on September 18, the day before the battle. When nothing happened on that day, they went home because their enlistments had expired; the next day, while they were walking away, the battle was fought.

The day after Freeman's Farm, General Burgoyne made preparations to resume the attack. He scheduled it for September 21, but on that date he received a message from General Sir Henry Clinton in New York City. The note indicated that Sir Henry was planning a move up the Hudson against the American forts on the river. The projected attack on Bemis Heights was canceled. There ensued a delay lasting over two weeks. This decision to wait was just wishful thinking. Clinton had promised nothing more than a diversion; with the forces at his disposal and considering the great distances involved, there was little more he could offer.

While waiting, both armies strengthened their positions. The Americans occupied and fortified the hill to the west of their original entrenchments. If the enemy tried to take this hill now, they would meet with a very different reception. Burgoyne, while waiting for news of Clinton's advance, laid out and had his army fortify the ground across the ravine to the north. Trenches were dug, earthworks raised, trees chopped down to provide a field of fire, and strong redoubts erected. The two most important of these near the west end of the line were known as the Breymann Redoubt and the Balcarres Redoubt, named for the officers who commanded the troops occupying them.

During this waiting period the strength of the British-German army dwindled to only about 5,000 effectives, with the men on half-rations and the horses starving. By contrast, the Americans rapidly gained in strength as volunteers came in ever-increasing numbers. General Lincoln, who had been operating on the east side of the river, harassing points along the British line of communications, brought his men over to the west shore.

Finally Burgoyne could wait no longer. Every day brought increasing hunger with no relief in sight. He was continuously losing men to American sharpshooters lurking in the woods around his camp. Positive action must be taken to relieve the situation. A council of war was called. Some officers advised retreat but Burgoyne insisted that he must make one last effort—but what to do? Very little was known about the American position. No scouts had been able to get through the woods to take a good look at it. Why not send out a large reconnaissance in force? Perhaps the Americans had not yet fortified the hill at the western end of their line.

With 5,000 men fit for duty, Burgoyne chose to send 1,600, almost a third of his army, forward on reconnaissance. This decision was obviously a compromise between hazarding a full-scale battle, and the sending of a small, fast-moving detachment capable of striking swiftly and then beating a quick retreat. Like most military compromises, it was a serious mistake. Such a sizable force invited a concentrated attack, but it was far too small to withstand an assault by a large portion of the American army.

On the morning of October 7, the British-Hessian reconnaissance force moved forward from the right end of the British line, and then halted in a wheatfield, while their leaders consulted as to their next move. This was an open invitation to attack, for, of course, no group as large as 1,600 men could hope to avoid being seen by the American scouts. The British position in the wheatfield was reported to General Gates, with the additional information that there were thick woods at each end of the line which would provide perfect cover and concealment for surprise attacks.

General Gates sent Morgan's rifle corps to swing wide through the woods to attack the British right; Poor's brigade went forward to make a simultaneous attack against the British left. The latter, having a shorter distance to advance, launched its assault first, followed soon thereafter by Morgan's men. Both ends of the enemy line recoiled from the shock, but the center still held fast.

Learned's brigade was approaching the field of battle when suddenly a horseman wearing an American major general's uniform dashed onto the field, placed himself at the head of Learned's column, and led the men forward, cheering wildly. Benedict Arnold had been completely unable to sit quietly in his tent listening to the noise of battle. With no authority whatever, he swept onto the field. Every man in the American army must have known that Gates had divested Arnold of his right to command, but here was a leader they wanted to follow. The first assault upon the British center was repulsed, but the second met with greater success. The enemy began to fall back.

There was on the battlefield that day another officer who wielded tremendous personal influence. In utter disregard of his own safety, Brigadier General Simon Fraser of the British Army was trying to stem the tide, riding back and forth along the line, urging his men by voice and example to stand fast. Drawing inspiration from their courageous leader, his soldiers had repulsed the first assault. Now, General Fraser, almost single-handed, was halting the retreat. Encouraged by his presence and conspicuous bravery, little groups were forming; under his direction a new defensive line was taking shape.

General Arnold and Colonel Morgan, the architects of American victory, regretfully decided that, if the attack were to succeed, this gallant British officer must go. Morgan selected a noted marksman named Tim Murphy to perform the task. At Murphy's third shot General Fraser fell mortally wounded, and with his fall the heart died out of the resistance.

The reconnaissance in force had failed completely. The great majority of the American victors were probably congratulating themselves upon their success in driving their enemy back into his entrenchments when, suddenly, they discovered that their day's work was not yet done. General Arnold saw that now, while the enemy might be disorganized by the retreat, and while the Americans were flushed with victory, would probably be the best chance anyone might ever have to assault and seize the British works, turn Burgoyne's line completely, and leave him vulnerable to attack from the rear.

Some other American troops were coming on the field.

Gates had not ordered them forward; their officers, following in Arnold's footsteps, had come of their own volition. Placing himself at their head, Arnold led them against the Balcarres Redoubt, but the defense was too strong there. Undaunted, Arnold decided to try again at another point. He saw Learned's brigade off to his left. To the surprise and horror of all present, he clapped spurs to his horse and galloped straight across in front of the Balcarres Redoubt, between the lines of the opposing troops firing at each other. To the utter amazement of all present, he emerged unscathed, shouted to Learned's men to follow him and charged with them straight between the Balcarres and Breymann Redoubts.

This attack was completely successful. It burst through between the two redoubts, whereupon Arnold turned his attention to the Breymann Redoubt. Here, Colonel von Breymann found himself attacked on three sides; other Americans were in front and Morgan had made a wide detour through the woods to attack from the outer flank. The Americans stormed the redoubt, swept through the *abatis* and over the parapet. Sword in hand, Arnold had circled to the rear of the fort to ride through the entrance. There, as he led the way, victorious, his horse was shot and he was downed with a bullet in the same leg that had been hurt at Quebec. Almost at the same moment Colonel von Breymann fell mortally wounded in defense of his post. With darkness closing over the field the Germans made an attempt to regain their fort, but were repulsed. The Battle of Bemis Heights, sometimes called the Battle of Stillwater, or even the Second Battle of Freeman's Farm, or Saratoga, was over.

The worst thing that ever happened to Benedict Arnold was to be only wounded in the Breymann Redoubt at the Battle of Bemis Heights. If the German soldier who fired at him had aimed a little higher, and Arnold had been killed, he would now be enshrined in the hearts of his countrymen as one of their greatest heroes. Instead of his treachery at West Point, he would be remembered by such names as Fort Ticonderoga, Quebec, Valcour Island, Freeman's Farm, Bemis Heights.

Although Horatio Gates was the nominal commander of the American army in upper New York when these last two battles were fought, there is no question that Arnold, ably seconded by Morgan and others, won these battles. What might have happened at Freeman's Farm if Arnold and Morgan had not gone out to fight in the woods in front of the American defensive position is difficult to say. On the other hand, if Gates had seen fit to answer Arnold's pleas for reinforcements at that battle, Freeman's Farm could have been a smashing American victory. The news of Burgoyne's surrender to a much larger American army at Saratoga impressed the world, but if it had come earlier as the result of an American victory after a battle fought with approximately equal numbers, it would have been startling news indeed.

Burgoyne's reconnaissance in force toward Bemis Heights was so poorly planned that it was doomed to failure. If Arnold had not dashed out onto the field, the battle would probably have ended with the retreat of the enemy force into its entrenchments. Eventually then Burgoyne would have retired from his position. But with Arnold's storming of the Breymann Redoubt, resulting in the complete exposure of the British flank and rear to attack, the enemy general had to leave immediately. Again the persistent thought recurs that, if Arnold had been the army commander, the full American force might have been employed from the beginning of the battle, the redoubt captured much earlier, the next redoubt taken, and the British placed in such a position that they could not have retreated. The result could have been as startling as if Freeman's Farm had been a smashing victory.

At the Battle of Bemis Heights, Burgoyne lost about 600 men killed, wounded, and captured. The Americans had only one-fourth as many casualties. In this battle a few other American units took a comparatively minor part, but for all practical purposes, the troops engaged were the same as at

Freeman's Farm: Morgan's riflemen and Dearborn's light infantry; Poor's New Hampshire and New York brigade with two Connecticut militia regiments attached; and Learned's Massachusetts and New York brigade—85 percent Continental soldiers.

On the next day the Americans occupied Burgoyne's camp, and it is an odd coincidence of history that, in some skirmishing which followed, Gates' other major general, Benjamin Lincoln, was also wounded in the leg.

With the battles over, the victories won, the enemy in retreat, the only problem the Americans now faced was to be sure that the British and Germans did not manage to escape. Both sides knew that there was little chance for the defeated army. It was the story of the retreat from Concord repeated on a much larger scale, with no hope for a relieving force in sight. With every passing day additional volunteers came to the American camps. Gates made good use of these men who, though they could not engage the British in the open field, were quite capable of conducting effective guerrilla warfare, harassing and sniping at the departing troops, delaying the retreat at every turn. General Stark came back to do his part by blocking the escape route to Canada. Surrounded by 20,000 men, Burgoyne surrendered. The formal ceremony occurred on October 17, 1777. A total of over 5,700 men laid down their arms. The great announcement brought France into the war. Spain came later, and eventually Holland was also at war with England. The American Revolution had reached its turning point.

5

Sir Henry Clinton Meets
the American Regular

Eight months to the day after the Saratoga surrender the British army began the evacuation of Philadelphia. For the Americans encamped at Valley Forge it had been a more miserable winter than the one preceding it at Morristown. Those who had survived the first would have been ready to predict that nothing could possibly exceed the rigors of the Morristown winter. Valley Forge had proved to be so much worse that comparisons were odious.

Yet from its ordeal the Continental Army had emerged stronger than before. The troop strength was greater than at the beginning of the winter when some of those sent to Saratoga had been returned. Then it had been about 11,500. Now it had increased to nearly 13,000, though during the worst of the winter's suffering it had dropped to less than 6,000 starving, emaciated souls.

The addition of numbers was, however, only a small part of the change that had been wrought in the American army. For the first time in its existence there was a standardized drill. Previously some units had been trained by British methods, others by French systems, still others by Prussian drill regulations. There had been no uniformity at all. Units depended entirely upon whatever system their officers might have learned. Regiments from different states varied in size. Yet, in spite of these variations, the officers and soldiers had done extraordinarily well during the past year. Nevertheless, Washington could not have been satisfied with the results. He knew that, if he was ever to have a real army with all its component parts functioning smoothly together, standards must be set and a uniform system established.

Washington himself could not possibly have undertaken the task of establishing a set of drill regulations, and then trying to institute and supervise a training program in addition to his other duties as commander-in-chief. Then, in February, there had arrived in the camp at Valley Forge another one of those foreigners. Far too many of these people had proved to be more trouble than they were worth. All too often American agents abroad had promised fortune-seekers high rank, which Washington could not give without superseding qualified Americans. When this new man, Baron Friedrich Wilhelm von Steuben, arrived, General Washington could not help but wonder whether he was getting another worthless adventurer or, if luck was on his side, a capable officer like the Marquis de Lafayette, the German de Kalb, or the Polish patriots Thaddeus Kosciusko and Casimir Pulaski.

When the newcomer arrived Washington reserved judgment, but not for long. Von Steuben, though handicapped by a lack of knowledge of English, undertook the task of preparing a training program for the army with such boundless enthusiasm and energy that Washington was delighted. It soon became apparent to von Steuben that he was dealing with a different type of soldier than he had known in Europe. These people in America were more individualistic; a simple copying of the drill regulations of a European country would not utilize their native abilities to the utmost, nor would the linear drill system fit conditions of warfare in the colonies. Something new would have to be added.

Von Steuben invented new model drill regulations, using the Prussian methods of Frederick the Great as a starting point, but greatly modified and adapted to fit the American temperament. He had to write this out in longhand, in French; then it was translated for him into English. Meanwhile, as each day's lesson was written, he began teaching it to the new army. At these sessions he set the example of personal teaching by demonstration. The soldiers of his first model company became instructors for the whole army. He taught officers that their duties were not limited to command in battle. He placed greater responsibilities upon the shoulders of junior officers than was the custom in the British Army. Noncommissioned officers must prove themselves to be leaders in all respects or be displaced. In three short months he welded a new spirit and a new confidence into this army. Many of the officers and soldiers had proved themselves brave and competent in several battles. Now, at last, they had an established system known to all, in which had been drilled.

The Marquis de Lafayette's name is better known today than that of General von Steuben. Yet the latter undoubtedly contributed far more to the combat ability of the American army than the French nobleman. The United States owes a great debt of gratitude to von Steuben.

As the Continental Army marched out to battle in the spring of 1778, one of its most cherished memories was of von Steuben on the drill field, shouting at them in French or German because his English was inadequate to the occasion, then pleading with his aides to swear for him in English. Von Steuben could feel justifiable pride as he watched his men going forward, determined to prove to the world that trained American soldiers were second to none.

While this reformation was occurring in the Continental Army, their opponents, living a life of ease in Philadelphia, had acquired a new commanding general. Sir William Howe had tendered his resignation. King George III had accepted it and ordered Lieutenant General Sir Henry Clinton to take his place.

The new British leader took command in the last days of May, 1778, with orders to evacuate Philadelphia, return to New York, then discontinue active campaigning in the north and undertake operations to recover the southern colonies. This was a complete right-about-face. Neither General Howe, who was leaving, nor Clinton, the new commander, had recommended such a radical change in policy. The decision had come from London and was based only partially on the fact that the war in the northern colonies had been a failure to date. King George III had no intention of giving any of the rebellious colonies their freedom but France's entry into the war had changed the situation drastically. The French fleet was powerful. Both England and France had colonies and naval bases in the West Indies. The London planners decided that it would be a tremendous task indeed for the Royal Navy to operate against the navies of France and simultaneously support a land campaign in the northern colonies, whereas it should be somewhat easier to support an invasion of the southern colonies, because Georgia and the Carolinas were closer to the West Indies. Furthermore, there were supposed to be a large number of Loyalists down south, eagerly awaiting an opportunity to join His Majesty's forces.

Before Sir Henry Clinton could make plans for an invasion of the southern colonies, he first had to evacuate Philadelphia and return to New York City. At the beginning of the Revolution, General Clinton might have considered such a movement a very simple problem, but now, with France in the war, communications by sea were more vulnerable. A French fleet could appear while the convoy was enroute; England no longer had complete control of the ocean. Also, General Clinton had more than his army and his baggage to transport. The Loyalists in Philadelphia had welcomed the British with open arms. Sir Henry Clinton had too much humanity in his soul simply to sail away and leave them to the tender mercies of the rebels. The Loyalists would therefore also have to be evacuated and there were not enough transports available to carry the army, its baggage, and the Loyalists too.

Unless the evacuation were to be effected in two convoys, using some of the same ships twice, thereby offering the French fleet at least three opportunities to attack the ships enroute, some of the movement would have to be made by land. However, General Clinton did not look upon the idea of a march across New Jersey with complete equanimity either. In the three years that had elapsed since he had arrived in Boston Harbor in company with Generals Howe and Burgoyne, he had acquired a grudging respect for the fighting ability of Americans under certain conditions.

Clinton's military education had been thorough, proper, and entirely orthodox according to the standards of the British Army. At a very early age he had received a commission as a lieutenant in the British Guards and, as the years passed, had worked his way up to the rank of major general at the age of thirty-four, with some battle experience to his credit during the Seven Years' War in Europe. At Bunker Hill he had, quite properly, recommended a landing in the rear of the Americans. This was the natural, logical approach which should have been adopted, but Clinton was overruled. He was given no assignment in that battle but, like Burgoyne, watched its progress from Boston. The two were equally horrified by the failure of the first and second assaults, but while Burgoyne stayed in Boston and continued to watch, Clinton took action. He crossed the water and joined the final successful assault as a volunteer.

One year later Sir Henry found himself in command of the army portion of an expedition assigned to seize and capture Charleston, South Carolina. He landed some troops on the island adjacent to Sullivan's Island, but then was unable to cross. Boats ran aground on the shoals between, but when his men tried to wade across, they stepped off into holes seven feet deep. The army was forced to stand helplessly by while the naval bombardment of Fort Sullivan failed. Although the naval commander, Admiral Sir Peter Parker, was primarily responsible for this fiasco, Clinton received a large share of the blame.

This stain on his military reputation was completely removed by the part he played two months later at the Battle of Long Island. There he was placed in charge of the advance elements of the army which swung around the American left flank and scored such an overwhelming success. On two other occasions during the year 1776, General Howe placed Clinton in charge of important operations requiring careful planning and professional ability. It was Clinton's division which landed first on Manhattan Island and it was Clinton who was dispatched to seize Newport, Rhode Island. Both operations were successfully accomplished with little difficulty.

Thus far in his career, except where naval reconnaissance of the water off Sullivan's Island had played him false, General Clinton's career had been uniformly successful. On every other occasion when he had been entrusted with an important command requiring technical proficiency he had accomplished the mission assigned carefully, competently, and skillfully, showing a professional ability of a high order. There had been no brilliant maneuvering, no flashes of genius, but his duty had always been done well.

At Bunker Hill his recommendations, based upon strict military logic, had been ignored, with disastrous results. In the year 1777, he advised General Howe to go to the aid of Burgoyne and again his recommendations were ignored, with disastrous results. While Howe's Philadelphia campaign and Burgoyne's Albany campaign were underway, Sir Henry had been left in command at New York with no specific orders to go anywhere. The troops under his command were too few to force their way up the Hudson to meet Burgoyne, but regardless of this fact, General Clinton became worried over the latter's safety and wrote to him, offering to make a demonstration on his behalf. In reply, Burgoyne sent a message urging an immediate advance. The messenger did not get through, but Clinton did not wait for an answer. He advanced up the Hudson, captured Forts Montgomery and Clinton seven miles below West Point after a brief but spirited struggle, sent a raiding party farther up the river, and then halted. A diversion was all that he had promised, but it had come too late in any event.

From this brief review of General Sir Henry Clinton's war

record it may be concluded that he would make his plans for the movement back to New York City with care, caution, and efficiency, and such was indeed the case. There were tremendous quantities of supplies to be loaded onto the ships or placed in wagons to be hauled overland. Three thousand Loyalists had to be safely put aboard the transports. Some of the troops were also scheduled to go by sea. Most of the army, a total of 15,000 men, were to make the overland march. Some were already on the Jersey shore, but the majority were garrisoned in or near Philadelphia.

The evacuation began on June 16, 1778, and was very skillfully executed. On the morning of June 18, word came to Washington that the British were gone from the city. The American army, knowing Philadelphia was being evacuated, might have tried to attack while some of Clinton's men were crossing the river. It is possible that a good opportunity was missed here, but it would have been a risky endeavor and Washington decided correctly not to chance it against such an opponent, who would surely have made provisions to guard against just this sort of attack.

Then for seven long weary days both armies trudged toward New York. The thermometer climbed to above 100 degrees, the humidity rose, and frequent rainstorms drenched the troops, but failed to break the heat wave that held New Jersey in its grip. Both armies suffered intensely, but the effect on the men in the British and Hessian ranks, who were carrying packs weighing from 60 to 80 pounds, was appalling. Some were so overcome that they staggered to the side of the road and died where they fell. Nor was the heat the only problem. The march was continually harassed by Continental troops and by the New Jersey militia detailed by Washington to snipe at the column, obstruct the roads with fallen trees, and burn the bridges over every creek. Having to clear these roads and rebuild the bridges in this intense heat, so that the immense baggage train of 1,500 heavily laden wagons could proceed, made progress painfully, depressingly slow. General

Clinton had hoped to reach his destination without fighting a major battle, but the Americans, marching on clear, unobstructed roads, without heavy packs, had been making more rapid progress. His line of march and that of the Americans on his left (west) flank were converging. Therefore, on the eighth day, June 25, Clinton turned his British-Hessian army away to the northeast, hoping thus to avoid a battle. Unfortunately, though, there was only one road leading in the new direction. Previously his troops had been marching on two approximately parallel routes. Now they were all strung out along one road, presenting a much more vulnerable target if the Americans could march fast enough to catch them.

Judging solely from General Clinton's actions one might think that everyone in the American army was pressing forward eagerly to attack the retreating column on the march across New Jersey. Such was not the case. There were two entirely conflicting schools of thought on the subject. On June 17, while the British were in the process of evacuating Philadelphia, General Washington had called a council of war. At this meeting several officers, including Greene, Lafayette, and Wayne, had urged an attack as soon as a favorable opportunity occurred.

Others, influenced by Washington's second-in-command, General Charles Lee, suggested that the best course to pursue would be simply to let the enemy go away as fast as possible. Lee argued that no Americans could stand up to the bayonets of the trained British regulars. At the beginning of the war General Lee had been appointed one of Washington's senior major generals because he was an experienced, professional, ex-British officer who could be expected to advise Washington on military matters. The advice that General Lee gave at this conference on June 17, 1778, would have been entirely proper back in 1775 or in 1776. But in the last three years of active warfare the Continental Army had gradually become an army in fact as well as in name. The officers were no longer amateurs; neither were the troops, who were ready to prove to von Steuben that they had mastered their lessons. General Lee, whose opinion, unfortunately, was still highly regarded in some circles, had been absent all during the year 1777 as a prisoner-of-war. He had been captured just before the Battle of Trenton and had therefore not had any opportunity to observe the continued American improvement in battle efficiency at Brandywine, Germantown, or Saratoga. Nor had he been present during the winters at Morristown or Valley Forge. He simply had no idea what kind of an army the Continental Army had become, or what sort of men served in that army.

As a result of the council of war Washington had compromised. He had called on the New Jersey militia to harass the retreating enemy and obstruct their passage, and had sent some of his Continentals out ahead with the same mission. Later, not entirely satisfied with his own compromise, Washington had detached additional troops from his main column to hang on the retreating enemy's flanks and rear. Brigadier General Anthony Wayne was the senior officer present among all these detachments, but it was decided at a conference that a major general should be detailed to coordinate the efforts of all these units which had, by degrees, become a force of considerable size.

The command of the advance forces was first offered to General Charles Lee, as a matter of courtesy, because he was the senior major general. He contemptuously refused the offer. Lafayette accepted the command with delight. By this time the change in Clinton's line of march had become known to the Americans, and Lafayette was anxious to try an attack on the rear of the long, meandering column. He hurried forward with enthusiasm to take command.

Then General Lee changed his mind. He had discovered that the advance guard, including the various attached militia units, was so large that it included nearly one-half of the army. Lee demanded that he be given command by virtue of his seniority. This was most embarrassing to Washington. Lafayette would be terribly disappointed, but worse than that, with France in the war, the Marquis was no longer just a simple volunteer. Unofficially he represented France and that country might be offended by the replacement of their representative at such a critical moment. Fortunately, Lafayette had acquired a tremendous respect and admiration for Washington. He immediately understood the dilemma in which his commander-in-chief had been placed and magnanimously volunteered to serve under General Lee's command in any capacity.

Lafayette's prompt action thus saved everyone from tremendous embarrassment, but Washington must have had other qualms about assigning Lee to command. In the last months of 1776, during the retreat across New Jersey after the fall of Fort Washington and just prior to the Battle of Trenton, General Charles Lee had acted in a very peculiar manner. He had completely ignored Washington's repeated orders to march immediately to join their forces. Apparently he had made other plans and considered his judgment in the matter far superior to that of his commander-in-chief. Then, fortunately for the American cause, Lee had been captured. General John Sullivan had assumed command of Lee's men and promptly marched to join Washington. With his own, Sullivan's, and other troops, Washington had then achieved the near-miracles of Trenton and Princeton.

Perhaps Washington thought, or hoped, that his second-in-command had learned his lesson and would now obey orders. Whether such was the case or not, there was another objectionable factor involved. In the recent conferences Lee had vehemently opposed making any attack upon the retreating army, although it was obvious that Washington favored taking action if presented with a good opportunity. Now, with the enemy forced to move in one long, thin column upon one road, circumstances seemed more than favorable. Could Washington trust Lee to carry out his orders with energy and enthusiasm when Lee's heart was not in the project? It is a matter of record that, on June 27, Washington gave orders to General Lee to attack Clinton's rear guard when it began to march the following morning. (By June 27, the advance guards of the American army had managed to get within striking distance of the British.) Washington left the details of coordinating the attack to Lee's discretion, but made it quite clear that, if the attack on the British rear guard proved profitable, the whole American army would be brought into action. It is also a matter of record that General Lee then did nothing more than call his officers together, inform them that the situation was indefinite, promise some sort of action on the morrow, and then go to sleep for the night.

Now General Clinton had actually reached Monmouth Court House on June 26, but then had been forced, because of the utter exhaustion of his troops, to remain there all the next day. That was why the Americans had been able to catch up to the British. However, having rested his men on June 27, Clinton was anxious to start moving again. At four o'clock in the morning, General von Knyphausen's division began marching. The baggage trains were to follow these troops; next would come Cornwallis' division, leaving a rear guard to protect the column. General Clinton decided to march with Cornwallis, whose division was larger than that of von Knyphausen.

As far as the British and Germans were concerned there was nothing to indicate that June 28 would be different from any of the other days they had endured since leaving Philadelphia. It was going to be another scorcher, with the thermometer again rising above 100 degrees and the humidity excessive. There had been a severe rainstorm the day before but it had not cooled the air in the slightest. About five o'clock in the morning some firing had broken out about a mile toward the west. This sort of skirmishing was so normal an occurrence that neither the troops nor their officers paid much attention to it. Some four hours later, after von Knyphausen and the wagon train were well on the way and Cornwallis' troops had begun their march, some more firing occurred, but again it attracted little attention.

Then at about 9:30 A.M., large bodies of American troops began appearing beside the road north of Monmouth Court House. By 10:00 A.M., there were enough troops gathered there to threaten the safety of the rear guard. General Clinton immediately realized that at least some of the units of the main American army were present. These must be driven away before the march could be resumed and it would take a lot more than just the rear guard to drive them back. Hastily Clinton gave Cornwallis orders to turn his division about and prepare for battle. Cornwallis' men, who numbered some 9,500, could quickly disperse the Americans and the march could then continue. Von Knyphausen, with his division, was to proceed onward with the baggage train. Then, to the British commander's complete surprise, the Americans after a few feeble efforts to attack, began to retreat. Whatever the reason for the sudden withdrawal, Clinton saw that it was far too good an opportunity to miss. He promptly gave orders to Cornwallis to pursue and destroy the enemy.

There was no way in the world that the British commander could have guessed why the Americans were retreating. The Continental troops, who had at last caught up to their enemy, had begun to prepare for battle in high spirits. At last, after all those weary days of marching in the terribly hot sun and drenching rain, the enemy was in sight. Their officers had led them out to form a line ready for battle but there had been an extraordinary amount of unnecessary confusion. The problem was simply that no one had prepared a plan of battle or taken charge as the situation developed. General Lee had issued a few unrelated orders, and then had contradicted some of them. As the orders were passed down the chain of command and were met by contradictory instructions, brigade and regimental commanders in line next to each other found their units assigned entirely different missions. Some units formed for attack; others began to retreat. General Lee seemed

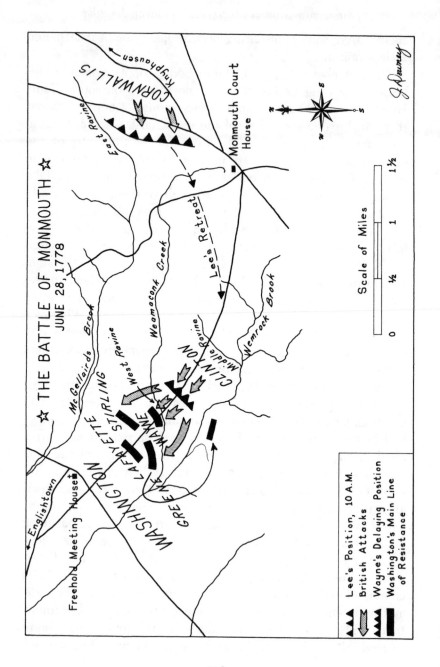

☆ THE BATTLE OF MONMOUTH ☆
JUNE 28, 1778

CORNWALLIS

Knyphausen

Monmouth Court House

Lee's Retreat

East Ravine

Weamaconk Creek

Wemrock Brook

Middle Ravine

CLINTON

West Ravine

WAYNE

STIRLING

LAFAYETTE

GREENE

WASHINGTON

McGellairds Brook

Freehold Meeting House

Englishtown

Scale of Miles

0   ½   1   1½

Lee's Position, 10 A.M.
British Attacks
Wayne's Delaying Position
Washington's Main Line
of Resistance

J. Downey

quite pleased by developments. Perhaps he believed that his point had been proved: Americans were not yet trained to face British bayonets. So the retreat began, some units marching back in pursuance to orders, others simply following, with Clinton and Cornwallis in pursuit.

At this point Sir Henry Clinton and Lord Cornwallis were delighted with their excellent progress, but they were also slightly puzzled. The Americans had been retreating rapidly for two miles, but there were no muskets or other articles of equipment littering the roads or fields. There was none of the normal evidence of a disorderly retreat. Then suddenly, just after the leading British had crossed a creek called the Middle Ravine, the Americans swung about and halted. This was extraordinary. The British generals were amazed. They knew full well that only very highly trained, disciplined soldiers could be stopped and turned around in the midst of a retreat, in the confusion and uproar of battle, with a pursuing enemy right at their heels. To attempt such a maneuver with poorly disciplined or partially trained troops would have resulted in utter ruin. Yet these American faced smartly about like veterans. Volley fire thundered from their ranks.

The British generals had no way of knowing what had caused this sudden turn of events. The halting and turning of the American army was due to the sudden timely arrival of General George Washington on the field. In a towering rage the commander-in-chief ordered Lee to the rear. Washington had been given reports that the army was retreating but, at first, had refused to believe them. Then, riding forward to the sound of the guns, he had finally become convinced. Enroute he had selected a defensive position behind the West Ravine, ordered the main body to deploy there, then galloped forward to find Lee and, if possible, stop the army before all control of it was gone.

Lee's dismissal took but a moment. Then, at Washington's personal command, the troops wheeled about. Anthony Wayne took charge. He and other gallant officers hastily organized an intermediate position to delay the pursuers as long as possible until Washington could organize the main defensive position behind the West Ravine. The officers and the men occupying that intermediate position knew that there was little chance of stopping the British attack with such a hastily organized line, but they hung on grimly until forced backward by repeated assaults. Slowly they gave way, foot by foot, across the West Ravine; then Wayne halted them again just in front of the center of Washington's new main line of resistance.

Sir Henry Clinton had now committed his troops to the battle. The flower of the British Army was on the field. Initially Cornwallis' division had been turned about only to save the rear guard and, of course, the wagon trains. That had been easily accomplished; Von Knyphausen and the army's baggage were now miles away, perfectly safe. But then the strange American retreat had begun. To turn the retreat into a rout had looked so easy, but his hasty pursuit of a disorganized foe had suddenly turned into a large-scale battle in which the British were forced to continue the assault. To halt the attacking troops would be almost the same as admitting defeat. The battle must go on or British prestige in the colonies would be shattered. The word would spread rapidly that the regulars, including the British Guards, had been halted, stopped dead in their tracks, by this Continental Army of the Americans.

General Clinton saw that the troops on the American left flank were still getting into position. Hoping to catch them before they were fully ready, he launched an attack. Nine months before, at the Battle of the Brandywine, General Sullivan's men had been caught in the same precarious situation and been driven from the field. This time von Steuben's training paid tremendous dividends. The defenders swung smartly into line to meet the assault. A bitter struggle lasted on that flank for nearly an hour until a sudden American attack rolled Clinton's troops backward.

Against the other wing Clinton hurled a second assault, but here the attackers ran into an enfilading fire from a position on their left. Even the British Guards could not stand against the withering gunfire being directed upon them by artillery and muskets from both front and flank. Another attack on Wayne's troops in front of the center of the line also failed.

General Clinton was now in a most unenviable position. As commander of a hitherto invincible army, he had unexpectedly encountered far more vigorous resistance than he had dreamed possible. Throughout history other generals have placed themselves in somewhat similar positions, and in most cases acceptable solutions have not been found. In almost all such instances the enemy resistance encountered came as a disagreeable surprise. If, at the beginning of the campaign, the enemy had been evaluated at his true worth, the generals concerned could have avoided placing themselves and their armies in such situations. Unlike Generals Howe and Burgoyne, Sir Henry Clinton had recognized the fact that the Continental Army had become a formidable foe, but he had not thought it capable of such continued bitter resistance over such a long period of time.

The British assault against the American right wing had failed. The attack on the opposite wing had also been forced backward. Yet General Clinton felt that he still had to make one more effort; his troops of which he was so proud might yet succeed. Military history is filled with examples of generals who, faced with similar situations, have called upon their soldiers to make one final, gallant charge to save the day. There are so many historical parallels that might be drawn that a list would be unduly long. Two of the better known, taken from more recent history, will suffice. At Waterloo, Napoleon Bonaparte had made successive attacks for eight hours against Wellington's troops. He could have retreated but a victory at Waterloo was his only alternative to utter ruin. He threw in the famous

Old Guard at the center of the British line. In the greatest battle ever fought on American soil, General Robert E. Lee had been partially successful on the first day of Gettysburg. On the second day, in an attack on the other flank of the Union army, the assault had almost succeeded. Finally, on the third day, feeling supreme confidence in the valor of his men, he launched Pickett's Charge at the center of the line.

General Clinton at Monmouth waited an hour to organize his forces for the final assault. When the attack came it was aimed directly at Anthony Wayne's position in front of the center of the line. The charging British troops were far too numerous for Wayne's men to halt. He and his soldiers fell back on the main position but, having forced Wayne to retreat, the attackers could make no further headway. The main line of resistance was now far too strong for Clinton's courageous, but exhausted, troops to pierce.

Washington would still have liked to organize a counterattack but darkness prevented it. By the next morning Clinton and the British army were safely on their way to New York. Both sides could with fairly equal justification claim a victory. The British had driven the Americans back, prevented an attack upon their marching column, and held possession of the major part of the battlefield until after dark. The Americans, on the other hand, had, after Lee's inglorious retreat, repulsed every attack, and the following morning were in complete possession of the entire battlefield.

The 9,500 men in Cornwallis' division had lost about 350 killed, wounded, and missing, of whom 59 had died from heat exhaustion. Almost all of Washington's Continental Army took part in the battle: about 12,500 troops plus about 800 New Jersey and some Pennsylvania militia, a total of some 13,500 men. The total American losses were almost exactly the same as those of their opponents, including 37 who had died from sunstroke.

Many historians have chosen to label the Battle of Monmouth Court House as indecisive. It is true, of course, that neither side won a clearcut victory. General Clinton and his army went on to New York. The British fleet, with its convoy of troops and Loyalists, also arrived safely just a few days ahead of the French fleet. Washington established his army in the Hudson Highlands.

General Charles Lee, whom many were now openly accusing of treachery, wrote some bitter letters to Washington and ended by asking for a court-martial. Washington quite properly placed Lee in arrest and preferred charges against him. The court found him guilty on almost all counts, but the sentence was remarkably light—suspension from command for one year. After a long delay the Continental Congress approved the sentence. At a later date Lee wrote an insulting letter to the Congress, which then informed him that his services were no longer needed.

But what was the effect of the battle on the British forces now safely in New York? First, it may be observed that they were right back where they had started from after the capture of that city in the summer of 1776. Two years of campaigning had resulted in no gain at all as far as the main British army was concerned. The only other city in British possession in the northern colonies was Newport, Rhode Island, which Clinton had captured early in December, 1776, shortly before the Battle of Trenton. Late in July, 1778, in an attempt to make some use of the French fleet which had appeared in northern waters, Washington suggested that a combined load and naval expedition be sent to recapture Newport. The attempt, made in August, failed.

Both sides now settled down to a war of attrition and therein lies the proof that the Battle of Monmouth Court House was not indecisive. Back in 1776, the British leaders were planning how to win the war in the north against an army which, if they could only catch it, they could surely defeat. Now, after Monmouth, neither Clinton nor any of his more intelligent officers were so sure they wanted to catch it, unless they had superior numbers on their side. This would be very unlikely since they were under orders to send a large share of their troops to the south. Therefore, none of the British leaders in New York made any plans for offensive moves in the north that might result in having to fight a major battle. They suspected that the Americans who had proved so thoroughly capable in a defensive situation at Monmouth might be just as effective in the attack. Throughout the remainder of the year 1778, the British leaders did nothing more than send out some raiding parties.

Meanwhile, Sir Henry took action to comply with the orders from London to send troops to the West Indies and also to invade the south. He dispatched 5,000 men to the West Indies and then 3,500 to Georgia. The latter expedition overwhelmed the small American force which tried to stand in its way and captured the city of Savannah with ease. Another British force from Florida joined it, and Augusta, Georgia, fell soon thereafter. Major General Benjamin Lincoln was sent to take command of the southern department. His efforts to recover Georgia, in the spring of 1779, failed, but an event was about to occur in the north which would confirm General Clinton's worst fears concerning the offensive ability of the American Continental Army.

6

Anthony Wayne
—Discipline and Bayonets

With the coming of spring in the year 1779, the Continental Army's primary mission was still to watch the main British forces occupying the cities of New York and Newport. Although the British commander, General Sir Henry Clinton, had sent 5,000 troops to the West Indies and 3,500 British, Hessians, and Tories to invade the State of Georgia, the bulk of the British Army forces were still concentrated in the New York area. General Washington was compelled, therefore, to continue to maintain the greater part of his army in the northern colonies. He could do little to aid the south in its efforts to resist invasion.

However, for the first time since the beginning of the Revolution, Washington felt that his army was strong enough to undertake a large-scale punitive expedition against the Indians, so long as the troops were not committed at too great a distance from New York City. To date, the local settlers had been forced to take care of themselves as best they could, relying primarily upon their own resources. As a result they had been tormented frequently throughout the war by savage Indian raids.

One outstanding success had been scored against the Indians and the British agents who aided and abetted them. In the spring of 1778, Lieutenant Colonel George Rogers Clark, a Virginian who had moved to Kentucky, then a county of Virginia, had organized a small expedition which had accomplished wonders. Starting from the vicinity of present-day Louisville, he and his men had descended the Ohio River, and then turned northward into Illinois and Indiana. In a nine-month campaign lasting until late February, 1779, involving almost unbelievable physical hardship, wading shoulder-deep in icy water in the depth of winter to surprise his enemies, Colonel Clark had seized control of a large portion of the country north of the Ohio and east of the Mississippi. Although bitter fighting then persisted along the frontier until the end of the war, this region remained in American hands and, at the peace conference, the Old Northwest Territory was ceded to the United States.

Colonel Clark's brilliant operations were conducted at too great a distance from New York City for Washington's army to lend a hand. However, a number of Tories and their Indian allies had conducted several devastating raids in western New York and Pennsylvania including, in 1778, terrible massacres at Wyoming Valley (Wilkes-Barre, Pennsylvania) and at Cherry Valley (west of Albany, New York). Washington and the Continental Congress decided that these shocking outrages must be avenged, and that the distances involved were not too great to prohibit the use of Continental troops. A total of 3,700 men were placed under the command of General John Sullivan to march against the Six Nations. While this expedition was getting underway, General Sir Henry Clinton organized an expedition of his own to move up the Hudson River.

Whether or not General Clinton knew that a large segment of the Continental troops had been withdrawn from the New York City area for an expedition against the Indians, he proceeded with caution. In the last days of May, 1779, he assembled at the northern end of Manhattan Island a force of 6,000 men, and provided a fleet of seventy ships and a large number of boats. On May 30, the troops climbed aboard. Two days later, on June 1, they landed on the west shore of the Hudson at Stony Point, and at Verplanck's Point opposite it on the east shore of the river.

At these two places, small American forts were being esta-

118

blished. Fort Lafayette at Verplanck's Point had been completed; work on the fort at Stony Point was still in progress. Both were garrisoned by only a handful of soldiers and both were captured in short order. The British hastily began construction of a much more powerful fort at Stony Point.

Now it seemed a little strange that General Clinton should make such elaborate preparations and commit such a large force as 6,000 troops just to capture these two forts about thirty miles upriver from Manhattan Island, unless he had some more ambitious project in mind. Washington naturally had to act on the assumption that this move might be only the prelude to an attempt to seize West Point, the most important position in the Hudson Highlands, less than fifteen miles farther up the river.

It would be a real triumph for British arms if they could capture West Point. The importance of having strong fortifications at this place where the river narrowed and turned had been recognized at the very beginning of the war. As early as 1775, a fort had been built on Constitution Island opposite West Point. Then really extensive fortifications had been begun, early in 1778, under the direction of Colonel Thaddeus Kosciusko. Fort Clinton, built on the cliff commanding the bend in the river, had already been completed.*
Fort Putnam, named for General Israel Putnam in command

*This Fort Clinton, later used for many years by the cadets of the United States Military Academy as their summer camp, should not be confused with the Fort Clinton seven miles downstream, which, together with Fort Montgomery, had been captured and then abandoned by Sir Henry Clinton in his 1777 diversion to aid Burgoyne. The name Clinton appears so often in New York history as to be confusing. The British commander, Sir Henry Clinton, was the son of George Clinto, a former royal governor of New York. Then there were two famous American brothers, George and James. Both were brigadier generals, and George was the first American governor of the state of New York, a position to which he was reelected six consecutive times. Both had participated in the unsuccessful defense, in 1777, of Fort Clinton (named for the governor) and Fort Montgomery (named for General Richard Montgomery killed at Quebec). George had been in overall command of the defense, James in direct command at Fort Montgomery. At this time James, the father of the later Governor De Witt Clinton, was preparing to take part in Sullivan's punitive expedition against the Indians.

at West Point, was almost finished, together with several out-lying redoubts.

To ensure the complete safety of West Point, Washington hurriedly ordered additional units of the Continental Army into position north of Stony Point, but no further British advance was attempted. Gradually it became apparent that Sir Henry Clinton had no intention of penetrating farther into the Hudson Highlands. Why then had he committed such a large number of troops on such a minor foray? Nearly a year had passed since the Battle of Monmouth Court House, but during that entire period the British had confined their activities in the north to raiding expeditions, hit-and-run affairs not designed to secure and hold any definite objectives. However, this expedition to Stony Point fell into an entirely different category. It was not a raid; the British had come to stay. The purpose was to establish permanent control over an important section of the Hudson River. In the process they might encounter sizable portions of that Continental Army which had conclusively proved its effectiveness at Monmouth. Therefore, to guarantee success, large British forces were assigned to the project to remain in the area until Stony Point could be converted into a really strong defensive position. When this was done, Stony Point and Verplanck's Point were left with adequate garrisons. The mobile forces were withdrawn toward New York City, but only partway. They were established in camps within close supporting distance at Philipseburg, now Yonkers.

By this venture General Clinton extended British control about thirty miles upriver and interrupted communications on the main highway between New England and the other colonies. Supplies and troops which previously had crossed the Hudson at King's Ferry, between Verplanck's and Stony Point, would now be forced to move by a longer route around to the north. This was most annoying to Washington, and also Stony Point was uncomfortably close to West Point.

Now there had been under consideration for many months a plan to form a corps of light infantry, composed of specially selected officers and men, chosen from the entire Continental Army for their physical energy, courage, and ability. Back in the days of the Brandywine Campaign, when Washington had sent Daniel Morgan and his expert riflemen northward to help stop Burgoyne, a special light infantry unit had been organized to take the place of Morgan's rifle corps. Under the command of Brigadier General William Maxwell the light infantrymen had performed outstanding service at Brandywine and again in the Monmouth Campaign. Because these soldiers had proved so useful, Washington decided to organize a special élite unit.

There were at least three outstanding officers who might logically have been assigned to command the corps, equivalent in size to a brigade. They were General Maxwell, Colonel Morgan, and Brigadier General Anthony Wayne. Maxwell had already been selected to command a brigade in Sullivan's expedition. This left Morgan and Wayne. Either would surely have been more than acceptable, but the unit was to be armed with muskets and bayonets. Colonel Morgan was more experienced in the type of operations that might be expected of this new corps, but he had almost always commanded primarily rifle units. Washington therefore chose Anthony Wayne who, he knew, was also anxious to obtain the coveted position.

For the sort of work in which the light infantry corps immediately became involved, Brigadier General Anthony Wayne was undoubtedly the right man for the job. The mission, of course, was to attempt the capture of Stony Point and the plan for doing so, as it was evolved, would require exact timing, courage, vigor, and the enforcement of strict discipline.

Generally speaking, when people mention the storming of Stony Point, a mental picture immediately arises of a wildly daring, perhaps even foolhardy venture, executed in the

121

middle of the night with bayonets only, conceived somewhat on the order of a buccaneering exploit. And the man who led it is remembered as "Mad Anthony" Wayne, so christened for his vigor and reckless daring in battle.

Some of all these elements were undoubtedly present but there is a great deal more to the story, which is ignored in this fanciful image. To understand what really happened at Stony Point we should start by taking a look at the man who was responsible for the success of this unique, daring exploit. Of all the general officers of the Continental Army who became famous in the American Revolution, Anthony Wayne would most probably have chosen an army career for himself. At a very early age he showed an unusual interest in military affairs, and if the United States Military Academy at West Point had been in existence, he undoubtedly would have applied for admission. Shortly after the war broke out he was placed in command of a battalion of Continental infantry recruited from his home state of Pennsylvania. (He had been born very near the town of Paoli in Chester County.)

In the spring of 1776, after the disastrous failure of the American expedition against Quebec, Colonel Wayne and his regiment had been among the reinforcements ordered northward. At the Battle of Trois Rivières they had fought gallantly, against greatly superior numbers, and then had taken part in the long, dreary retreat back to Fort Ticonderoga.

At the Battle of the Brandywine, Brigadier General Wayne had been left in command of the defense at Chadd's Ford after the departure of the reserve American division, which had been moved over to the right wing to help slow down Cornwallis' flank attack. Though heavily outnumbered by von Knyphausen's men advancing across the creek in front, he conducted a vigorous defense until suddenly struck by the British Guards, who emerged from the woods at the right and rear of his line. Yet, in spite of this unexpected attack, Wayne had managed to disengage his almost surrounded command and retreat in good order under cover of darkness.

Then, on the night of September 20, nine days after his very able efforts to defend the crossing of the Brandywine, General Wayne was given the bitterest lesson of his life. His troops were concealed in a woods near Paoli, very near where he had been born. He was contemplating an attack upon the enemy when, in utter darkness, General Charles "No-flint" Grey burst into his camp to kill and disperse Wayne's men. Not a shot was fired by the enemy; bayonets only were used. It was a lesson in warfare that Wayne was never to forget. General Grey's method of attack and the precautions taken by him to ensure such an overwhelmingly satisfactory surprise were impressed indelibly on Wayne's memory.

Anthony Wayne's participation in the Battle of Germantown has already been described. In this battle his troops were encouraged to avenge the so-called Paoli Massacre. Assuming that General Wayne was learning lessons from each of his encounters with the enemy, here he certainly learned that a plan must be practical and workable; if it contains the seeds of failure, they will surely germinate.

Finally, at Monmouth, Wayne and his men had been the heroes of the day. Over the years of combat he had learned the vital importance of discipline, drill, and training. On this battlefield he had taken personal command of the troops who had turned an inglorious retreat into a defiant battle for the army's existence. Perhaps no one else emerged from this conflict as thoroughly convinced of the absolute necessity of careful training and strict discipline as did Wayne. He had seen men who had previously disliked, even feared, the bayonet use it as effectively as any of their opponents who claimed it as their principal weapon. He had commanded and led the men who had smartly wheeled about, responding to their hours of drill, and stopped the charging enemy with well-aimed volleys. Now if he could only be given the chance to demonstrate the capabilities of these Continental soldiers in an attack.

Therefore, when Washington chose him to command the

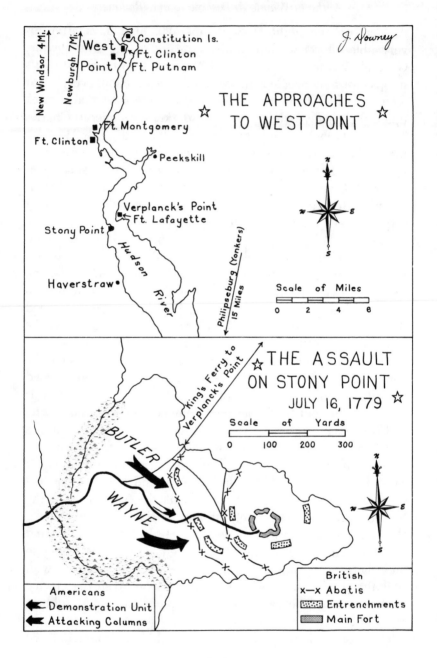

J. Downey

THE APPROACHES TO WEST POINT

New Windsor 4 Mi.
Newburgh 7 Mi.
West Point
Constitution Is.
Ft. Clinton
Ft. Putnam
Ft. Montgomery
Ft. Clinton
Peekskill
Verplanck's Point
Ft. Lafayette
Stony Point
Hudson River
Haverstraw
Philipseburg (Yonkers) 15 Miles

Scale of Miles
0   2   4   6

THE ASSAULT ON STONY POINT
JULY 16, 1779

King's Ferry to Verplanck's Point

Scale of Yards
0   100   200   300

BUTLER

WAYNE

Americans
Demonstration Unit
Attacking Columns

British
x—x Abatis
Entrenchments
Main Fort

124

corps of light infantry and told him to make a reconnaissance of Stony Point, General Anthony Wayne leaped at the chance. Perhaps, though, when he took a good long look at the position, he may have had some misgivings. Stony Point, and Verplanck's Point opposite it, each projected into the river, narrowing its channel between them. Stony Point was the larger of the two. It was really a peninsula extending out into the river for nearly half a mile. Near the tip of the peninsula rocky crags rose some 150 feet above the water, but at the base beside the mainland there was a swamp that was flooded at high tide so that the peninsula then became an island. At low tide the footing in the swampland would be treacherous and slippery; at high tide the only possible approach was over a narrow causeway.

On this high, rocky promontory the British had erected several batteries partially connected by trenches. Other log and earth embankments had been built at intervals around the main fort. To further strengthen the position, a curved line of interlocking tree trunks and limbs, with their branches sharpened, pointing outward, called an *abatis*, had been staked out, across the peninsula. Between it and the mainland were three more log and earth embankments protected by another line of *abatis*, through which an attacker would have to struggle. The garrison consisted of 600 men, commanded by Lieutenant Colonel Henry Johnson of the British Army, a reliable officer chosen to command this important post.

It was obvious at a glance that the garrison could hold out indefinitely against a siege as long as it could continue to be supplied by ships sailing on the river. The only possible way to take it would be by a surprise attack, but Anthony Wayne reported to Washington that he thought it could be done.

Washington agreed, although many of his advisors were certain that there was no possible chance of success. Then, although Wayne was completely responsible for the ultimate success of the attack, Washington offered several suggestions in writing, and discussed many of the details. On one such occasion, Wayne is supposed to have exclaimed, "General, I'll storm hell if you will plan it."

There was one point on which Washington saw no necessity to coach Wayne and that was on the choice of the troops to make the attack. Every soldier who was to take part in the assault was to come from the corps of light infantry, each a carefully trained, well-drilled Continental Army regular. A total of approximately 1,350 men were to take part. In addition, for several days ahead of time, Major Henry Lee's horsemen were to watch every avenue of approach to guard against spies or reconnaissance parties. Then, before the approach march was made, every dog was disposed of so that no barking would alert the defenders.

At Washington's suggestion, the attack was scheduled not for the usual time just before dawn, but instead the hour selected was just after midnight. Each man was to have a piece of white paper in his hat and a watchword was to be announced. Strict silence was to be observed throughout the approach until the troops actually reached the enemy lines, when every man was to begin shouting "The fort's our own!" One version of the story is that this was actually the British countersign for the night, and had been obtained for the Americans by a slave who, for several days, had been allowed to enter the fort and sell strawberries to the garrison.

The attack was to be made in two columns. General Wayne was to lead the right, somewhat larger, force on the south side of the causeway. Colonel Richard Butler was to lead the left column to attack north of the causeway. In front of the right column there was to be a detachment of 150 volunteers equipped with axes in addition to their muskets and bayonets. Their mission was to chop openings in the *abatis*, through which a lieutenant and 20 men were to rush to engage the enemy. In front of the left column there was to be a similar detachment of 100 volunteers; a lieutenant and 20 men were also provided here to pour through the openings as soon as possible. None of the men in either of these columns were to use anything but the bayonet. Muskets were not to be loaded. Any soldier who attempted to load his musket was to be instantly killed by his officer. General Wayne was a strict disciplinarian and everyone knew it. Yet there is an account that one man didn't believe he really meant it. When this man started to load his musket his captain instantly ran him through with his sword.

One unit, however, did have loaded muskets. It was not to take a direct part in the initial assault, but was to move toward Stony Point on the causeway. When the British gave the alarm this unit was to start firing to mislead the defenders as to the point of the attack.

Seldom has a plan worked so perfectly, but seldom has a a plan been so carefully prepared and executed by such thoroughly trained troops. On the morning of July 15, 1779, the troops were lined up, inspected, and all equipment carefully checked. At noon they began their thirteen-mile march to the fort. Just before midnight all the men were in their assigned positions and the slow, silent advance began. It was not until the soldiers were almost to the first line of *abatis* that their presence was discovered—first Wayne's right column, then Butler's left column. At the first sounding of the alarm the American unit in the center, on the causeway, began a continuous firing with their muskets.

The enemy reaction was rapid, possibly too rapid, because half the garrison was rushed down toward the causeway where the demonstration was being made. Yet to right and left the defenders' fire took its toll. Axemen went down, so did the men tearing their way through the openings. Those coming behind also fell. But not a shot was fired by the Americans in the attacking columns. General Wayne was hit by a bullet which creased his skull but only temporarily stunned him. Helped to his feet by two of his men, he rejoined the attack. As often occurs after a famous battle, peculiar legends inevitably arise. It is hard to believe that Wayne, thinking he was mortally wounded, asked to be carried into the fort, and that his soldiers charged forward with their commander on their shoulders.

From beginning to end, this brilliant, daring exploit, requiring the utmost in skill, courage, and determination, lasted only half an hour. All honor is due to each of the brave men who took part in the assault and, at the end of the attack, there occurred another remarkable demonstration of the, discipline that had made it possible. There was not a single instance reported of any enemy soldier being wounded while trying to surrender. When the Continentals were ordered to halt, the command was instantly obeyed. As one senior British officer put it: "The rebels had made the attack with a bravery never before exhibited, and they showed at this moment a generosity and clemency, which during the course of the rebellion had no parallel." General von Steuben would have been very proud of his soldiers.

The American loss was 15 killed and 80 wounded. The British had 63 killed in action and 543 captured, of whom 70 were wounded. At daylight on July 16, Wayne opened fire upon the fort across the river at Verplanck's Point but with no apparent result. There had been a scheme to make a simultaneous attack upon this fort also, but it had not taken place. General Clinton hastily rushed reinforcements to the British garrison and canceled a raid that he had planned against New England.

The news of the storming of Stony Point spread over the country like wildfire and undoubtedly lost nothing in the telling. "Mad Anthony" Wayne's name was on everybody's lips. The British were astounded and dismayed to learn that such a completely successful bayonet attack had been made upon their regular troops. General Sir Henry Clinton had been given a defiant answer to his unspoken question—were these American Continentals, who had proved so capable in defense at Monmouth, as effective in the attack? The British commander had been criticized for being overly cautious in dealing with these rebels; now, in his opinion at least, his judgment had been vindicated.

It would be interesting, but of course impossible, to discover how many of the American colonists mentally classified Stony Point as another battle similar to Bunker Hill, in which free men had again shown their superiority to the British regular. Undoubtedly there were many who did not stop to think that the New England farmers and townsmen who fought at Bunker Hill could not possibly have achieved the victory at Stony Point.

Certainly Sir Henry Clinton and the majority of the British and Hessian officers and soldiers recognized the difference between the men of 1775 and the soldiers of 1779. Certainly, also, Washington and most of his officers and men of the Continental Army were well aware of the distinction. All they had to do was recall the unsanitary campsites around Boston, the complete lack of training there, and then compare these memories with the efficient soldiers who, operating under the strictest discipline, had taken Stony Point. The army had come a long, long way since the days of the so-called officer who was the company barber at Boston. Yet many of the same individuals could have, and probably did, fight at both Bunker Hill and Stony Point. The difference was not in the individual; it was training and drill that had made him a capable, reliant soldier.

Judging only by the reaction of the people of the United States after the war, there were far more who failed to differentiate between the two types of soldiers than there were who appreciated the vast gulf that divides the brave but untrained fellow from the courageous soldier worthy of the name. The lesson was there, plainly written, for all to read. But it was an unpopular lesson and there were some supposedly qualified individuals who were yet to prove, before this war was done, that they were incapable of understanding, or applying, what they should have learned.

Most people naturally assume that, as a result of this

brilliant exploit, the Americans retained possession of Stony Point. The exact opposite occurred. Washington inspected the position and decided that it would take too many men to garrison it. The Americans then removed all the captured guns and supplies and abandoned the post. Sir Henry Clinton promptly reoccupied it. This fact does not detract in the least from the significance of the battle. The combat ability of the Continental Army had been thoroughly demonstrated. Stony Point was a great moral victory and the effects of that moral victory were felt very soon.

One month after Stony Point, Major Henry Lee attacked another British garrison at Paulus Hook, now a part of Jersey City. His exploit was not as spectacular or as successful as Anthony Wayne's but he captured a large portion of the garrison and helped to keep the enemy worried about the safety of all his outposts.

The attack on Stony Point occurred in July and had been followed by the raid on Paulus Hook in August. In the fall of the same year, 1779, when General Clinton was preparing to extend and intensify the British efforts in the south, he made a survey of the various locations his soldiers occupied in the north and remembered particularly the attack on Stony Point. He decided that the only way to guard against such assaults would be to evacuate everything but New York City. The British garrisons at Stony Point, Verplanck's Point, and all troops stationed at Newport, Rhode Island, were withdrawn. Such was the moral effect of the victory at Stony Point.

Much later in the war, after General Clinton had returned north and a French army had landed at Newport, when Washington was planning the Yorktown Campaign, the American commander-in-chief played upon Clinton's fears for the safety of New York itself to deceive the British general as to his ultimate objective. Such was the respect that the British commander had acquired for the American regular.

In the Yorktown Campaign, Anthony Wayne again displayed outstanding skill as a combat commander. We have paid particular attention to the careful manner in which he planned and executed a night assault, when he was given plenty of time to think about it in advance, but at Green Spring, Virginia, on July 6, 1781, he unexpectedly found himself the victim of a surprise British attack.

General Wayne had been sent southward with his Pennsylvania Continentals to reinforce the Marquis de Lafayette who was commanding the American forces facing Lord Cornwallis in Virginia. Shortly after Wayne's arrival the British troops had turned toward the coast. Lafayette's army was simply following behind. When it became evident that Cornwallis was about to cross the James River, General Lafayette thought he saw a chance to attack the British while they were in the act of crossing. He sent Wayne forward to attack what was believed to be only the rear guard.

Cornwallis had, however, laid a trap. Only a few of his men had crossed the river; the remainder lay hidden, screened by a small covering force. Wayne, thinking that the screening force was the rear guard he had been ordered to destroy, moved forward. The British retired slowly until Cornwallis gave the signal to send his entire army into battle. To Wayne's horror he found himself confronted by vastly superior numbers. With Lafayette too far away to render aid, with both flanks about to be enveloped, Wayne attacked with the bayonet. His quick thinking saved the day. Cornwallis and his troops were so surprised that they temporarily wavered. Wayne's attack was repulsed but the British had been thrown off balance just long enough for the Americans to conduct a rapid retreat. By his presence of mind and forceful action Anthony Wayne saved his command.

It is not surprising that in later years when Washington was President, and the new country was having a great deal of trouble with the Indians in the Northwest Territory, he should call on Major General Anthony Wayne. There had been two previous expeditions. The first had been a flat failure; the second had been completely defeated by a surprise Indian attack. In both cases the soldiers had been inadequately trained for combat. General Wayne set about correcting this condition. It took time, and he was criticized for his failure to take rapid action, but the result was the decisive victory of Fallen Timbers, August 20, 1794, won by a vigorous bayonet charge.

7

Horatio Gates—Politician-General

When the war shifted to the south its character was altered radically. The climate and terrain were totally different; the land was more thinly populated, the season for campaigning generally reversed; and the armies were much smaller. On both sides the veteran troops available for action were generally few in number so that American and British commanders were forced to rely heavily upon irregulars. The Loyalists played a much more important part in the southern war. A large number were imported from the northern colonies and, in addition, the southern Loyalists were far stronger and better organized. With so many Americans engaged on both sides, the war in the south was more truly a civil war, much more personal, more savagely, bitterly fought, in a far more violent, ferocious manner.

After the abortive attack on Charleston, South Carolina, in June, 1776, the south saw no large-scale action until the end of the year 1778, when a convoy from New York with 3,500 troops aboard appeared at the mouth of the Savannah River. The soldiers were British, Hessians, and northern Loyalists. The latter were not to be despised, for some of these native-born American units that fought for the crown were well-trained, efficient, and capable, comparable in quality to the British, Hessian, and American regulars.

To combat this army of 3,500, the colonists were able to bring less than 1,000 men into the field. As a result, the city of Savannah was easily captured. Soon another British force, from Florida, marched into Georgia. Late in January, 1779,

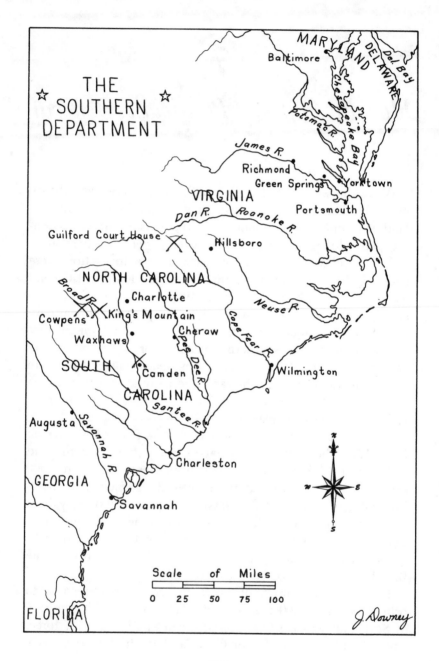

THE SOUTHERN DEPARTMENT

134

Augusta was also captured. The remnants of the American forces retreated to South Carolina, leaving Georgia in British hands.

In the course of the next four months Major General Benjamin Lincoln, who had been selected by the Continental Congress to command the southern department, made two attempts to recover part of the state of Georgia. Both attempts failed; the state remained under almost complete British control until near the end of the war.

During the hot summer months no important operations took place. Neither side felt strong enough to undertake an expedition against the other. Then in September, 1779, Admiral Comte d'Estaing, in response to an American invitation, appeared off Savannah with a large fleet and transports carrying 6,000 soldiers. When General Lincoln arrived with some more men, including Count Pulaski's Legion, the allies had such a preponderance of force that the city could have been taken with great ease, if an assault had been launched immediately. But d'Estaing wasted time delivering a formal demand for surrender, and then decided to undertake regular siege operations, which gave the defenders three weeks to strengthen their positions. When the attack was finally delivered it was repulsed at every point, with a loss of over 800 killed and wounded, including the gallant foreign volunteer, Count Pulaski. Admiral d'Estaing sailed away. Lincoln returned to Charleston. To date, French participation in the war had not been very helpful. The year before, after the unsuccessful attempt to capture Newport, relations had become somewhat strained between the colonists and France. This failure at Savannah did nothing to improve them.

With the approach of another winter, on the day after Christmas, 1779, General Clinton personally sailed south bringing a force of 8,500 British, Hessians, and Loyalists. Lord Cornwallis, now a lieutenant general, accompanied him as his second-in-command; General von Knyphausen remained in charge of New York City. The convoy ran into severe storms.

The ships were badly scattered. It took six weeks to reassemble them and land the troops thirty miles south of Charleston. By this time many of the horses had died, but the sufferings sustained by the troops on board ship were as nothing compared to the long, wearing march endured by the Americans who were simultaneously moving by land to reinforce South Carolina. The major part of the British-German army had remained in the New York City area. Washington was therefore forced to keep most of his army in that region also. However, he sent all the reinforcements he could spare, about 1,450 men. Naturally, he chose to send southerners to defend the south. Thus, the Virginia and North Carolina Continentals, who had previously trudged northward to fight in Pennsylvania, New Jersey, and New York, turned around and walked, through the dead of winter, hundreds of miles back south, all the way to Charleston to help defend that city.

By the time these soldiers had reached their destination, additional British reinforcements had been sent by ship to General Clinton from New York City. The Americans gathered to defend Charleston were heavily outnumbered, almost three to one. Now it certainly was the first duty of General Benjamin Lincoln to preserve his army for future operations. He should never have let it get cooped up in the city, but this is exactly what he proceeded to do. Of course, there were a few extenuating circumstances. Lincoln did not want to abandon the largest city in the Carolinas without at least a pretense of making a defense. He was under great pressure from the city authorities and the state government to try to save Charleston. The British advance was very slow, giving the Americans plenty of time to enlarge and strengthen their defenses. Apparently General Lincoln thought that he could stay to help defend the city, delay its occupation, and then escape at the proper time across the Cooper River, which ran along the eastern side of the city.

On April 10, 1780, Clinton called on the city to surrender. This summons was refused. Four days later the escape route was closed by a British lieutenant colonel of cavalry named Banastre Tarleton, whose name was soon to become very well known in the south. The troops he used to effect this closure were his own British Legion, composed of American Tories, Major Patrick Ferguson's American Volunteers, reinforced by two regiments of British regulars.

General Lincoln had stayed too long. Now there was no way out, although the siege lasted for another month. Finally, on May 12, the Americans laid down their arms. Over 5,400 men were captured, nearly 6,000 muskets, and over 390 guns. This surrender at Charleston was one of the greatest catastrophes of the war. The largest American army in the south was completely eliminated. Over 2,500 of the men surrendered had been Continental soldiers. Never again in the deep south would any American commander ever be able to assemble that many trained soldiers. The North Carolina and Virginia veterans of Brandywine, Germantown, Valley Forge, and Monmouth who had made that long march to try to save Charleston were gone.

As soon as the news of the surrender became known in South Carolina the little bodies of militia proceeding toward Charleston, with the hope of helping against the British, wisely and rapidly dispersed to their homes. This left one small body of Virginia Continental cavalry, only 350 men, in the entire state. On May 29, 1780, at the Waxhaws near the North Carolina border, this detachment was ruthlessly destroyed by Colonel Tarleton. Americans who tried to surrender, when they saw that resistance was hopeless, were slaughtered; the wounded, unable to move, were slashed and bayoneted; no mercy whatever was shown. Tarleton was a capable, energetic, brave officer, but insolent, vindictive and utterly ruthless, not at all a fair sample of a decent English officer. From this battle came the phrase "Tarleton's quarter," meaning a savage massacre of defenseless men.

The annihilation of this small American force ended all organized resistance in the state. Sir Henry Clinton returned to New York City, taking about one-third of his troops with him. Lord Cornwallis was left with 8,300 British, Hessian, and Tory troops to hold Georgia, complete the occupation of South Carolina, and then march northward and obtain control of the next state, North Carolina. At this time Cornwallis' assignment seemed easy. South Carolina appeared secure. Encouraged by the British victories, the Tories had risen. With their aid Cornwallis established strong garrisons at strategic locations throughout the state. American resistance appeared to have been overcome completely. The British commander began to lay his plans for a movement into North Carolina as soon as the worst of the summer weather should pass.

There were, however, a few more American soldiers marching southward. When Clinton had sailed from New York at the end of the year 1779, Washington had countered by sending some veteran North Carolina and Virginia soldiers to aid in the defense of South Carolina. Then additional British troops had been sent south by ship to join in the Siege of Charleston. When this second convoy had left New York City, Washington had released still more of his men to march southward to try to halt the invasion. Here, by the way, is a perfect illustration of the mobility afforded by command of the sea, as contrasted with attempting to march by land. The second contingent of American troops had barely reached the Virginia —North Carolina border when it received the news of the surrender of Charleston.

When this second group of veterans heard of the loss of the first group at Charleston, many among them must have wondered what was now to become of them. This second group, also southerners, numbered about 1,400 men. It was commanded by Major General Baron Johann de Kalb and consisted of two understrength brigades. The first brigade of four Maryland regiments was led by Brigadier General William Smallwood; the second brigade of three Maryland regiments and the Delaware regiment was led by Brigadier General Mordecai Gist. Both of these generals were well known, highly respected, and had proved their worth on many occasions, beginning as early as the Battle of Brooklyn Heights. There Gist had led Smallwood's Maryland regiment, which, together with the Delaware regiment, probably saved the army on Long Island from destruction. From that point onward there was hardly a battle fought by Washington's army in which they or the officers and soldiers who marched with them had not participated.

Were they also to be sacrificed, as had the preceding group of about 1,450 Virginia and North Carolina veterans before them been sacrificed? At least those who had preceded them had been marching to join other troops, South Carolina Continentals and a few Georgians. They were almost entirely on their own. They had been met by no one except Colonel Charles Armand with about 120 men, the remnants of Pulaski's Legion. The British, Hessians, and Loyalists in South Carolina vastly outnumbered them, over five to one. Yet they continued their march, expecting to meet some American militia who were supposed to join them but had not yet appeared. What Baron de Kalb might have done when joined by the Virginia and North Carolina militia will never be known, because a new American commander arrived on the scene.

When a new commanding general for the southern department was appointed, Washington's opinion was ignored. The Continental Congress chose General Horatio Gates, "the hero of Saratoga," whom they had originally appointed, in 1775, as adjutant general of the army with the rank of brigadier. This had been an excellent choice. Gates had served in the British Army, was an excellent administrator, and had proved extremely helpful to Washington in the early days before Boston when the commander-in-chief was working so hard to bring some sort of order out of the chaos that prevailed there.

Later, Gates, raised to the rank of major general, had been appointed Schuyler's second-in-command in the northern department. Unfortunately, there had been a misunderstanding at the beginning as to who was to be in command. It was resolved by Schuyler assuming the role of a theater commander while Gates took command of the troops. The only battle that had occurred was the naval Battle of Valcour Island fought by Benedict Arnold. During this campaign Gates' administrative ability had again proved helpful to the American cause, but Gates had been unhappy with his secondary role.

Near the end of the year 1776, General Schuyler had ordered Gates to take some troops to help Washington who was retreating across New Jersey. The men Gates brought took part in the Trenton-Princeton Campaign, but their commander avoided these actions. He went instead to visit his Congressional friends who had fled to Baltimore. This visit was the beginning of his eventually successful intrigue to replace Schuyler in command of the northern department. Fortunately, political scheming of this sort takes time. Therefore, General Schuyler had still been in charge during the early period of Burgoyne's invasion. Schuyler had been responsible for the adoption of the scorched earth policy which had paved the way for the ultimate British defeat. Benedict Arnold had directed the battles and Gates had emerged as "the hero of Saratoga."

During the succeeding winter a number of dissatisfied people began making unfavorable comparisons between Gates, who had won Saratoga, and Washington, who had lost Brandywine and Germantown. Such comparisons, based on emotion rather than logic, were, of course, inevitable and unfair. Washington, by his silence, ignored them. Gates, by his silence, condoned them. There is then supposed to have arisen a conspiracy to supplant Washington as commander-in-chief. This conspiracy became known as the "Conway Cabal." It was named for Thomas Conway, an Irish adventurer who had been appointed a brigadier general in the army. This conspiracy was always a mysterious sort of thing. Very little concerning it was ever definitely proved and eventually the idea of supplanting Washington simply collapsed.

However, the conspiracy may have left its mark upon Gates. In other words he may have become a victim of its propaganda: that he was entirely responsible for the victory at Saratoga; that he, not Washington, was the great American general of the Revolution. In this spirit, Major General Horatio Gates arrived in North Carolina late in July, 1780, to take command.

The situation that faced the new commanding general of the southern department should have been enough to give anyone pause, but Gates appeared completely confident. He seemed not in the least perturbed by the fact that Georgia and South Carolina had already been seized and were garrisoned by a force of 8,300 trained British, Hessian, and Loyalist troops, plus some southern Tories. To do battle with this enemy he had only Armand's Legion of 120 men and 1,400 Maryland and Delaware veterans commanded by de Kalb.

This is the way that General Gates should have reckoned the odds—1,520 American soldiers against 8,300 British, Hessian, and Loyalist soldiers stationed at various posts throughout the two states. Perhaps if Horatio Gates had counted the troops in this manner, he would have conducted an entirely different sort of campaign, using his 1,520 veterans as a nucleus around which the militia might gather. Separate attacks could then be directed upon some of the scattered posts when favorable opportunities occurred.

Such a campaign did not, however, appeal to General Gates. He had spent too many months criticizing his predecessor, General Schuyler, for giving up Fort Ticonderoga without a struggle, and then retreating again and again in front of the advancing enemy. Gates could not now adopt a similar policy. He must have immediate action with prompt results. To live up to his reputation he must advance, no matter what the odds.

Unfortunately, at this point, we cannot even give Gates credit for making a courageous decision to fight and die facing fearful odds because he had not stopped to analyze what had really happened in the Saratoga campaign. Because of his inability to do so, the officers and men of the Maryland and Delaware regiments would be called upon to respond to the question put by Horatius at the bridge: "And how can man die better than facing fearful odds . . . ?"

Horatio Gates had not been present on a battlefield, to see enemy bullets fired, for over twenty years, not since the French and Indian War. As a captain he had taken part in Braddock's expedition in 1755 and been wounded in the ambush. Like so many other people he may then have drawn the usual erroneous conclusion that regular forces in America could easily be defeated by the homegrown product without additional training. He had evaded the Battles of Trenton and Princeton and stayed in his tent while the Battles of Freeman's Farm and Bemis Heights were being fought. Undoubtedly Gates also had swallowed the publicity that followed the Battle of Bennington. He had completely failed to grasp the fundamental fact that Burgoyne's superior army had gradually been whittled down in size until it was approximately equal to the strength of the Continental forces, which had been reinforced by Washington. The militia had been very useful to Gates in the last days before the Saratoga surrender, harassing the retreating army, and blocking the road to Canada. He knew that Arnold had employed militia in battle but he had not been present to watch how Arnold had used them in conjunction with the Continentals, who strengthened them on each side and encouraged them by their presence. The fact that the battles had been fought and won primarily by veteran Continentals had not registered on Gates' mind.

Therefore, when Baron de Kalb informed him that there were over 3,000 militia in Virginia and North Carolina who were supposed to join the army, Gates did not hesitate to give orders to advance. Counting these 3,000, and making no distinction between trained and untrained soldiers, he was confident that his army could surely defeat the garrison of any British post. If such dire consequences had not resulted, one might be tempted to take pity upon the memory of General Gates. The last time he had come to take command of an army he had become famous. This time he was to leave in disgrace. There was no Schuyler to save American troops for later use on other fields by giving up a Ticonderoga; Lincoln had lost them all at Charleston. Gates was not facing a Burgoyne who would commit only a portion of his troops to battle; he was faced by a Cornwallis who was a far more aggressive leader. And Washington had no more regiments to send. Gates was on his own with 1,520 soldiers and perhaps 3,000 militia, and he did not know the difference between them.

Having ignored the basic military factors of training and discipline, Gates proceeded to ignore basic logistics. The men were practically without food; the State of North Carolina which was supposed to provide supplies had failed to produce any. The little army could not stay where it was because there was no more food obtainable in that region; foraging parties had already brought in all there was to be had. Since the army had to move one way or another, rather than retrace their steps back toward Virginia, Baron de Kalb and the other senior officers recommended an advance in the general direction of Camden, moving by a circuitous route over which some food supplies could be obtained. General Gates announced that this route was fifty miles too long; the army would take the shorter road. His officers who were acquainted with the region protested vigorously; the country was almost entirely barren of all types of supplies. Overriding these and all other pertinent objections, Gates ordered the army to proceed. The resultant march was a nightmare. All the worst predictions of the officers who knew the country came true. The only food obtainable was green corn, green apples and green peaches. The men had to eat in order to have something to fill their stomachs, and so came down with dysentery. Many dropped out from sheer exhaustion, though the the majority kept on because they had no other choice. Finally, terribly weakened by their march, they were joined by various groups of Virginia and North Carolina militia and obtained some small amounts of food.

The American army now numbered some 4,500 soldiers and militia, of whom only 3,450 were fit for duty. Sickness on the march had reduced the Maryland and Delaware soldiers to only 1,000 effectives. Armand's Legion had about 100 men. Only 2,350 of the militia were present and fit for duty. With this force Gates proposed to make an attack upon Camden, which he had been told was held by a garrison of something less than 2,000 men. At this juncture Gates received a message from Brigadier General Thomas Sumter, who commanded some South Carolina volunteers, asking for a loan of some men to help capture a British wagon train. Gates sent 400, including 100 of his Maryland veterans. This unnecessary diversion further reduced the combat strength of the Maryland-Delaware brigades to only 900 men. The number of trained soldiers at hand, counting Armand's 100-man Legion, was therefore only 1,000, with about 2,050 attached militia. Gates issued orders for a night march on Camden, beginning at ten o'clock on the night of August 15, 1780.

Of course, Lord Cornwallis had heard of the approach of the American army toward his post at Camden. He had sent reinforcements to the town and had decided to come in person to direct the battle. The total British-Loyalist force available for action, strengthened by these reinforcements, now numbered 2,250, most of whom were trained British or Loyalist soldiers. Only about one-fourth of Cornwallis' men were Tory militia. Thus, the American army outnumbered the British nearly three to two, but in trained soldiers the British outnumbered the Americans over three to two.

Hoping to surprise his enemy, Cornwallis also ordered a night march, beginning at the same hour, 10:00 P.M. To the complete surprise of both, the two met in the darkness north of Camden. Neither had much sleep that night. When dawn came the Americans, who had formed lines on both sides of the road, saw the British advancing toward them. They also discovered, as did the British, that the battle was going to be a head-on collision. There were swamps on both sides, allowing no room for maneuver. The position was sprinkled with thinly scattered pine trees.

During the hours of darkness, Cornwallis had formed his army for attack, placing the British regiments on the right (east) side of the road and the Tory regiments on the left of the road. The Tory militia were on the extreme left of Cornwallis' line. Thus the best units in the first line were on the right or east side of the road, the poorest at the extreme left. Lieutenant Colonel James Webster commanded the right half of the line. Lord Rawdon was in command of the trained Tory units on the left of the road and of the volunteer militia. In his second line, Cornwallis placed a regiment of Highlanders with the cavalry of Tarleton's British legion behind them, ready to exploit any advantage.

Gates' formation for battle was similar in that he also placed most of his best units on the right of the line. Of his 900 Continentals, 600 were on the right and the other 300 held in reserve. The North Carolina militia were in the center, the Virginia militia on the left, with Armand's Legion to their rear.

At dawn, August 16, 1780, the artillery on both sides opened fire. Since there was no breeze, the gunsmoke hung close to the ground and mingled with the gray haze of early morning. Partially hidden from view, their movements obscured by the haze and smoke, the British infantry deployed for action, advanced to within 50 yards, fired a volley, and charged with the bayonet. Some of the Virginia militia shot at the advancing redcoats. All took a look at the solid line of scarlet, saw those glittering bayonets, and fled for their lives. Who could blame them? They had never received any sort of training to prepare them for the appalling vision that had burst, unannounced, upon them. In their wildest dreams they had never imagined

☆ THE BATTLE OF CAMDEN ☆
AUGUST 16, 1780

1. Va. Militia
2. N. C. Militia
3. 600 Md. & Del. Continentals - Gist
4. 300 Md. Continentals - Smallwood
5. Armand's Legion

Scale of Miles

0   ½   1

GATES

Gum Creek

DE KALB

CORNWALLIS

Saunders Creek

Camden

A. Br. Regulars - Webster
B. Loyalist Infantry } Rawdon
C. Tory Militia
D. Highlanders
E. Tarleton's Cavalry

J. Downey

such a shocking sight as the sudden appearance out of the battle smoke of a line of British soldiers, the thunderous volley aimed at them from as close as 50 yards, and then the surging charge of yelling soldiers with lowered bayonets. They had nothing to hide behind; there were no entrenchments as there had been at Bunker Hill. Each man stood completely exposed, a perfect target for those naked steel bayonets.

Nor can anyone blame the North Carolina militia who stood beside the Virginians. They saw their neighbors disappearing into the woods behind them, took a look at those shiny bayonets, and, without firing a shot, ran off the field. In a matter of minutes Gates' army had been reduced from a strength of 3,050 men almost to the original 1,000 veterans, the only ones he should have relied upon in the first place. Worse was yet to come. Armand's 100-man Legion had been placed in the rear of the left of the line. In the wild flight these 100 were literally swept off the field by the fleeing thousands and with them went Gates himself, leaving General Baron de Kalb in command of what remained.

Some of the fleeing thousands had also blundered into the 300 Maryland Continentals in reserve. Though they tried to open ranks and let the men through, great confusion resulted, and a few of these veterans, including General Smallwood, the brigade commander, were violently separated from their comrades and shoved away from the battlefield. Colonel Otho Williams took charge of the brigade and, in response to a request for assistance from de Kalb, moved forward.

Meanwhile, what had happened to de Kalb and Gist's 600-man brigade? It had violently repulsed the attack of the Loyalists troops and Tory militia on its half of the field, then counterattacked and was driving forward, victorious. To exploit his victory, de Kalb had called for the reserve.

At this crucial moment, Lord Cornwallis swung the right of the British line to strike Williams' 300 men moving forward to help Gist and de Kalb, and committed his reserve to battle. Attacked in front, on the left flank, and in their rear, unable to get forward to reach de Kalb, the 300 were overcome by sheer weight of numbers. Forced to give ground, they were borne backward, stubbornly contesting every foot. They also were taken out of the battle.

Less than 600 Maryland and Delaware soldiers, plus one North Carolina regiment, were now left to face the entire enemy army. This one militia regiment is a remarkable example of what a little training and one leader can accomplish. The commander was Lieutenant Colonel Henry Dixon, a Continental veteran, who had taken advantage of a few opportunities available prior to battle to give his men a bit of training. When the British charge came, this regiment, next in line beside the Continentals, watched the men on their left flee but, inspired by the personal example of their colonel, and encouraged by the presence of the stalwart soldiers on their right, held their place in the line. Firmly they stood, with the 600, and awaited their fate.

Perhaps if de Kalb and Gist had been able to see what had happened on the rest of the battlefield, they would have been able to retreat, and have saved some of their men. But no word had come from Gates. The fog and smoke of battle had prevented them from seeing the wild flight that had occurred on their left. All they knew was that they had been counterattacking and winning the battle on their half of the field.

Now it was too late. They were hemmed in on all sides, front, flank, and rear, with a swamp at their backs. Yet they would not yield. In savage hand-to-hand, bayonet-against-bayonet fighting, the first attacks of the enemy were violently repulsed. Against odds of over three to one the Americans counterattacked and drove back the troops surrounding them. When these closed in again, they were once more repulsed. Against Cornwallis' entire army, the 600 fought on, the fiercest, most violent bayonet struggle of the entire war. With no thought of surrender the American resistance continued until Tarleton's cavalry was hurled against their rear and the resistless tide of overwhelming numbers engulfed them in front and flank. Baron de Kalb was captured, bleeding from eleven wounds, to die three days later. A few men escaped, some of them through the swamp, pursued by musket balls.

The British pursuit was conducted by Colonel Tarleton in his usual relentless, vicious manner for twenty miles. General Gates, of course, was perfectly secure. On a remarkably swift horse he had reached Charlotte, North Carolina, sixty miles away. Two nights later he was at Hillsboro, nearly 200 miles from the battlefield, where he planned to reorganize the army. It took the remnants of that army, led by Smallwood, Gist, and Williams, three weeks to wend their weary way that far back to be reorganized.

The Battle of Camden has been universally recognized as the worst defeat ever inflicted upon an American army in battle. The responsibility for this tremendous disaster rests equally upon the shoulders of General Horatio Gates, who proved beyond a shadow of a doubt that he was completely incompetent, and upon his political friends in the Continental Congress, who substituted their military judgment for that of Washington.

The British reported only 324 casualties in the battle. This figure is undoubtedly far too low. Perhaps it should be doubled. The furious nature of this bitter struggle must have produced heavier losses among the British and Loyalist troops, approximately equal to the losses suffered by the Continentals. The latter have been estimated as 650 killed, or captured wounded. In addition, about 100 American militia were killed and wounded, almost all of them from Colonel Dixon's gallant regiment. Some 300 other militia were captured, presumably by Tarleton in his pursuit. Therefore, the American battle casualties may be counted as 1,050 men, against about 600 British and Loyalists. However, to evaluate correctly the total effect of the Battle of Camden, we must now add to the American losses the thousands of militia who disappeared completely, homeward bound.

No country, no matter how good its military educational

system may be, will always produce good officers. Mistakes in selection will inevitably be made. When these mistakes are placed in command of troops on a battlefield, disaster may be the result. It is difficult to compare Horatio Gates with other soldiers in our history, but another who caused the needless death of good, trained men was George Armstrong Custer. Ignoring the orders of higher authority, he led his men into the Battle of the Little Big Horn in an effort to gain fame. In a way the motives of the two officers were similar: Custer was hunting for glory, Gates wanted to preserve the fame he had already acquired. Fortunately, there have been very, very few such officers in the history of the United States Army.

There is another category in which Horatio Gates definitely belongs. He was one of the first of a long line of American troop commanders who became victims of the legend that untrained Americans could defeat disciplined enemy troops, that patriotism and enthusiasm are all that are needed to win wars. There have been so many horrible examples in our history of the result of sending untrained troops into battle that it seems unnecessary to make even a partial list. Almost every country in the world has been taught this lesson at one time or another, and most established countries have taken their punishment and learned their lesson faster than the United States. For over a hundred years it looked as if this country would never absorb the teachings of history. The War of 1812 constituted an almost unbroken chain of military disasters until trained troops began appearing on the battlefields. The city of Washington was captured; the White House and the Capitol were burned. In this connection it may be noted that there is no other instance in recorded history where the capital of a great nation was delivered to the enemy after such small loss as that sustained at the Battle of Bladensburg in 1814, which preceded the capture of Washington.

Even this humiliation made little impression on the attitude of the people toward the necessity of maintaining adequate military and naval forces. Just forty-seven years later, in response to the public outcry for immediate action, a battle was fought near Manassas beside a little creek named Bull Run by troops wholly untrained for combat. The generals who were forced to fight this battle knew that the men were as yet untrained. The generals protested against the decision to march, but were forced to comply. After the battle was over, General Stonewall Jackson exclaimed: "Give me 10,000 fresh troops and I will be in Washington tomorrow." This was not a request. It was a wish that Jackson knew could not be fulfilled because the victorious Confederate army had also fought the battle with untrained men and, as a result, was almost as disorganized and exhausted by its victory as the Union forces were by their defeat. What Stonewall Jackson really meant was: "if I could be given 10,000 fresh troops"; he knew they were not available. But he clearly indicated what would have happened if the United States had been fighting a trained army at Bull Run.

To turn back to Horatio Gates, it should also be noted that, in one respect, he was unusual. Most American generals, unless they were themselves untrained, strongly objected to being forced to take men into battle with little or no drill or training. Also, in many instances, they became public scapegoats for the defeats which inevitably followed. As we have seen, Horatio Gates made no objection; in fact, he was eager to bring the militia into the Battle of Camden. Furthermore, after the disaster, he was treated kindly, courteously, and sympathetically by Washington and by Nathanael Greene, his successor, although Washington saw to it that he was never given another combat command.

In most of the battles waged by the United States with unprepared soldiers, the real victims have been the unfortunate men and boys who were committed to the slaughter. Here, also, Camden was an exception to the general rule. The militia left the battlefield so rapidly that most of them were never caught by the victorious enemy, who had to take time first to deal with the troops who stayed to fight. At Camden it was the Maryland and Delaware Continentals who were sacrificed on the twin altars of ignorance and blind prejudice against the military.

It was most unfortunate for the future of the United States of America that the true story of what happened at the Battle of Camden never became a matter of public knowledge. There are several obvious reasons why this was so. First, and perhaps foremost, people much prefer to talk about victories rather than defeats. Yet it is unquestionably true that we can often learn far more from our mistakes than from successful ventures.

Secondly, any study of the Camden battle would have disclosed the part the Continental Congress had played. It had paved the way for the disaster by selecting its political favorite to lead the army in preference to letting Washington, the commander-in-chief, nominate a suitable candidate. No one could question the right of the Congress to make such a choice whenever it saw fit. That was a prerogative which the Congress might exercise at any time it chose. Naturally, therefore, those responsible for selecting General Gates were not in favor of publicizing their error. Generally it seemed best not to press any investigation too hard, and just get on with the war. The safest way to cover up the mistake was to call on George Washington to retrieve the disaster, by asking him, at this late moment, to nominate a commander who might be able to save the south. It seems appropriate to mention here that several of the best men in the country who had served in the Congress in the early days of the war were no longer members in 1780. In many cases those who had succeeded them were by no means as capable.

In later years the Congress was naturally loath to resurrect the story of Camden because it conflicted directly with the American myth as to how the Revolution had been won. The fact is that the Battle of Camden provides the best illustration in the entire history of the United States of what may be expected from trained versus untrained men when subjected to the terrors of combat. The men who joined the militia regiments had as much natural courage as those who fought in the Continental regiments. If the militiamen had been sheltered by some sort of entrenchments, they would undoubtedly have stood their ground for a while at least. But when they saw those enemy bayonets each one thought of himself as an individual target, standing by himself. Each one could be certain that the men on his right and left would probably run; therefore, all ran together.

This left 900 soldiers to face 2,000. Later, there were only 600 against 2,000. Yet none of the 900, or any of the 600 left their ranks. The steadiness, resolution, and valor of the 600 at Camden should be as well known to every American as the courage exhibited by the 600 of the Light Brigade. Each did his duty and many died:

> . . . tho' the soldier knew
> Some one had blunder'd.

The reason they stood, and fought on, and died was simply because they probably were, and certainly considered themselves to be, the best trained units in the Continental Army. Fortunately for the United States enough escaped to continue the war and win back the south.

The worst defeat ever inflicted upon an American army in battle should be remembered not as a disgrace, but as an object lesson. Above all, the stand made by those veterans from Maryland and Delaware, and by Dixon's North Carolina regiment, against odds of over three to one, hemmed in on all sides, should be remembered with great pride. No soldiers of any other nation have ever fought more bravely.

8

Daniel Morgan's Classic Victory

Three weeks after the Battle of Camden, the remnants of the American army were gathered at Hillsboro, North Carolina. Here General Gates began a complete reorganization. It was a comparatively simple task as far as the personnel were concerned because there were so few of the Continentals left. The regiments had been understrength before the battle and so many men had been lost that several of the regiments were merged together. Although a few recruits came into camp, plus some survivors of the Waxhaws massacre, the net result was a reduction from the two understrength brigades which had fought at Camden to one understrength brigade and a small corps of light infantry, with a few attached cavalrymen. Some of the militia stopped in on their way home but continued on when they found very little food available, or were discharged because their terms of enlistment were about to expire.

There was very little Gates could do about the food problem, although he made every effort. The soldiers never saw a whole day's ration and considered themselves very lucky indeed if they received a half-day's ration. Almost all other supplies of every sort were gone and of course the men were not paid, and had not been, for a long time. When and if they received their pay they knew it would be practically worthless. The rate of exchange for Continental currency was somewhere between 60 and 100 to 1. It is most difficult to understand how these men survived, or how their families, many miles away, to whom they could send nothing at all, survived. Yet under these circumstances, and after the crushing defeat at Camden, it is reported that their morale was still high. Whenever we think of patriots in the American Revolution, the Continentals, their wives and their children, should stand head and shoulders above all the rest.

In direct contrast to the dire plight of the Americans, Lord Cornwallis brought additional troops to Camden and advanced toward North Carolina, completely confident that he would soon bring that state under British control. By this time a strong difference of opinion had developed between Cornwallis and his superior, General Clinton, in New York as to how the war should be conducted. Both had the same ultimate end in view, the suppression of the rebellion and the return of all Americans to British control, but the two generals advocated different methods of approach.

General Clinton was the more cautious of the two. He believed that the rebels could not maintain themselves forever. Their financial system was breaking down completely. He felt that the colonists were growing weary of the conflict, which had already lasted over five long years. He knew that the supply situation for the Continental Army was deplorable. Even the most patriotic of soldiers must surely succumb eventually with no supplies, little food, and no pay. His idea was that a continued series of devastating raids aimed at leading cities would in time accomplish the desired effect. Extensive land campaigns need not be conducted. Avoid all unnecessary risks. Keep New York City, Georgia, and South Carolina under firm British control; and then expand slowly but surely, when the time became ripe.

With this viewpoint, Lord Cornwallis was in distinct disagreement. He did not believe in waiting to see what would happen next. A victory should be followed up immediately while the rebels were still disorganized. All his troops were not needed to maintain control of Georgia and South Carolina. There were plenty of soldiers and eager Tories available to advance into North Carolina. In short, he advocated a vigorous, aggressive policy. Furthermore, Cornwallis had found ways and means to bring his ideas to the attention of the London government. In order to save time in the rendition of reports to London, General Clinton had given Cornwallis permission to write directly to London instead of sending everything through headquarters in New York. Naturally, Cornwallis had taken advantage of this arrangement to present his viewpoint and had received the blessing of the authorities.

Cornwallis moved northward in two columns. The principal force, under his direct command, seized Charlotte, North Carolina. The other column, operating farther to the west, was smaller, only about 1,200 men. It acted independently and was therefore more vulnerable, although this fact never seems to have been appreciated by Cornwallis. The commander of this detachment was Major Patrick Ferguson, an excellent soldier, and also the inventor of a breech-loading rifle, which may have been the first breech-loader ever used by troops in battle. The occasion had been the Battle of the Brandywine where Ferguson had been wounded and had lost the full use of his right arm. Like Tarleton, he had raised a unit of Loyalists, which he called the American Volunteers. Unlike Tarleton, he was not infamous for ruthlessness or inhumanity.

Advancing across the border into North Carolina, Major Ferguson became alarmed by news that the mountaineers of North Carolina, Virginia, and the future State of Tennessee were rising against him. Ferguson turned about, retreated to what he hoped was an impregnable position atop King's Mountain just across the South Carolina border, and called on Cornwallis for help, which failed to arrive on time.

The Battle of King's Mountain, fought on October 7, 1780, fits the American legend perfectly in every particular but one. Seeing their homes about to be invaded, each man had grabbed his gun. Then, assembled under their chosen leaders, they had marched out, filled with determination to expel the royal troops. All were superb marksmen. Everyone had been trained from boyhood to shoot, and shoot straight, but none had received any formal training whatever. They surrounded the enemy and attacked, moving forward Indian-fashion, from tree to tree. The enemy had no chance at all, although they defended themselves bravely enough. Major Ferguson was killed and his command wiped out completely—killed, wounded or captured, except for some 200 who had left camp that morning on a foraging expedition. At one stroke, 1,000 of the enemy were eliminated at a cost to the Americans of only 28 killed and 62 wounded. Then the mountain men, having successfully accomplished their purpose, quietly returned to their respective homes.

The one way in which this battle does not fit the American legend that untrained patriots defeated British regular soldiers is that there were no British soldiers in the battle. The only Englishman present was Major Ferguson. It was really a battle of Americans against Americans. In fact, it was almost a battle of untrained Americans against untrained Americans because 90 percent of Ferguson's command were Tory militia. The other 10 percent were Loyalist troops.

Therefore, although popular orators have often pointed with pride to King's Mountain to illustrate their concept of how the Revolution was won, the battle, unfortunately for the American myth, simply does not fulfill the requirements. Yet next to Bennington, it is the battle most often referred to as a wonderful example of how the disciplined soldiers of Europe were defeated in the Revolution. Now it is entirely possible that, if regular soldiers had been sent into this country, they might have met the same fate at the hands of those same hardy, self-sufficient mountaineers who could shoot so superbly and were such experts at cover and concealment in the hills which were their home. The reverse of course would also have held true. The mountain men would have had little chance against the British on a battlefield such as Camden. But neither happened. Therefore it is rather an unprofitable exercise in imagination to attempt to draw definite conclusions from events which never occurred.

Many historians have selected King's Mountain as the turning point of the war in the south. In a military sense this is certainly not true. Upon receipt of the news, Cornwallis temporarily halted his invasion of North Carolina. He had been told that there were 3,000 mountaineers and was guarding against their sweeping around to attack some of his scattered outposts in South Carolina. His troops, not having been involved, were in no way affected by the battle. They still outnumbered the Americans reorganizing at Hillsboro. Four months after King's Mountain the British were chasing the Americans across North Carolina as fast as they could go. The turning point would not come until the middle of March, 1781, five months after the destruction of Ferguson's command.

The victory at King's Mountain did, however, have a great effect upon the strength of the American resistance movement in the south. It has been pointed out that there were two types of soldiers in the American army in the north—the Continentals and the militia. In the south there was a third type of soldier—the partisan, almost as distinctly different from the ordinary militiaman as the regular soldier.

The Carolinas and Georgia were a much more sparsely settled region than the north and the people were more equally divided in their sentiment. The armies were smaller and therefore less able to control the general population. At the beginning of the war small bands were formed who fought viciously against each other, but after the unsuccessful British attack on Charleston in June, 1776, the patriots had completely gained the upper hand. The Loyalists (Tories) were suppressed and their cause apparently lost. Then came the British occupation of Georgia in 1779 and the capture of Charleston in May, 1780. The Loyalists were so encouraged by these victories that they rose and, with the aid of British troops, overthrew their enemies. Operating in small groups, section against section, sometimes family against family, the fighting was more personal and therefore often extremely bitter and savage. Tarleton's ruthless massacre at the Waxhaws did nothing to alleviate the situation. When the previously defeated Tories discovered they had the upper hand, many followed Tarleton's example, but the burnings, lootings, and killings were by no means one-sided.

After the capture of Charleston and the establishment of strong garrisons at various important places throughout the state, Cornwallis and the Tories were confident that they would have no further real trouble. All coordinated opposition seemed crushed. A few small groups of patriots were hiding out in the swamps, emerging from time to time to attack isolated detachments, but this was to be expected. The numbers involved were small, perhaps twenty-five or fifty to a group, rarely as many as one hundred men. It seemed fairly certain that eventually the partisan leaders would be eliminated one by one, their followers would grow discouraged, and the resistance movement gradually fade away.

In this estimate of the situation the conquerors did not evaluate properly the great courage and intense patriotism of the partisans. Commanded and inspired by resourceful, determined, gallant leaders, such as Thomas Sumter, Andrew Pickens, and the most famous of all, Francis Marion, known to friend and foe alike as "The Swamp Fox," the partisans kept alive the spirit of resistance, though faced with apparently hopeless odds. British regular troops were seldom involved in this endless struggle but the American Tories, troops and militia alike, had to be constantly on their guard against the swift, impetuous attacks of the American partisans who were liable to appear at any moment, and then disappear back into the swamps where they would be lost without a trace.

The American victory at King's Mountain brought not only encouragement to these partisans, but also additional volunteers into their ranks. For the first time their numbers became large enough to constitute a real danger to some of the established British posts. Expeditions were organized to seek out and destroy the larger bands. After one such attempt, Colonel Tarleton has been quoted as exclaiming that "the devil himself could not catch" Francis Marion.

Late in September, about the same time that Major General Benedict Arnold failed in his efforts to deliver West Point to the British, Colonel Daniel Morgan arrived in the American army camp at Hillsboro to take up the struggle again for the American cause. Morgan's reappearance at the front affords a striking contrast to Arnold's treason. Both had been passed over for promotion on several occasions. Throughout the war the Continental Congress had consistently demonstrated remarkably poor judgment when dealing with the officers of the army. Daniel Morgan was not the only one who had been practically forced to go on an inactive status in order to preserve his self-respect. John Stark, prior to his victory at Bennington, had resigned for the same reason. On one occasion, Generals Nathanael Greene, Henry Knox, and John Sullivan had all threatened to resign their commissions because a worthless foreign adventurer was to be passed over their heads by the Congress. Fortunately for all, the man was accidentally drowned, riding his horse off the edge of a ferry boat, thus averting the crisis. The list could go on and on and, at the top of the list, the most long-suffering of all, would be the name of George Washington.

Shortly after his arrival in the American camp, Morgan was at last promoted to brigadier general. Early in December, 1780, the new commanding general of the southern department appeared. At last the Continental Congress had decided to let Washington decide who was the best general for the job. Washington's choice was Nathanael Greene, the man whom he would have selected months before if the Congress had permitted him to make the decision.

The combined battle experience of the two new leaders, Nathanael Greene and Daniel Morgan, was a far cry from Gates' almost complete lack of experience. There was hardly a battle that had been fought by the Continental Army in which either Greene or Morgan had not taken an active part.

Unlike Gates, both realized what a tremendous task they were facing and, unlike Gates, one of the first things Natha-

nael Greene did was obtain an accurate count of his soldiers.
The situation was more than faintly reminiscent of the one
that Washington had faced in March, 1777, at Morristown.
In the army there were 2,450 men and, of these, only about
1,100 were Continentals. All were lacking clothing, equipment
and ammunition; food was also very hard to get.

With these 1,100, less than 70 percent of them physically
able to do duty, Nathanael Greene was supposed to hold
North Carolina and make a pretense of regaining South Carolina and Georgia. To wait with 1,100 soldiers to halt an invasion of North Carolina was to invite disaster. Eventually, whenever Lord Cornwallis was ready to move northward, he would
march with far more, and the 1,100 would have to retreat or
be overcome in battle.

The alternative to waiting in place was to advance and, at
first glance, this seemed equally ludicrous. This was exactly
what Gates had done; to repeat his mistake would mean inviting another Camden. There has been a great deal of discussion
about Greene's decision. In retrospect it is easy to say that he
did the right thing simply because it worked out all right,
but a great number of writers have failed to understand his
motives. They have assumed that he had an army of 2,450
men and generally base their discussions on this fact. If this
had been the case, Nathaneal Greene might not have divided
his army into two parts because, by doing so, he invited
destruction of each part in turn.

By his own count, General Greene knew he had only 1,100
soldiers on whom he could rely. It would be foolish to attempt to fight Cornwallis with this handful. Perhaps, though,
he could follow the example set by the partisans of fighting
in small groups. Thus, he decided to divide his little army into
two parts. He selected Brigadier General Daniel Morgan to
command one force while he went with the other. His own
destination was Cheraw Hill where he was joined by Lieutenant Colonel Henry Lee's Legion of 280 men and some 400

Virginia militia. Morgan's smaller army, which went farther westward, was also reinforced by over 300 militia.

Confronted by this division of his enemy's army, Lord Cornwallis proceeded to divide his own forces, not into two, but into three parts. He also had been reinforced after the Battle of King's Mountain and had a total strength of about 4,000 men, of whom over three-fourths were trained British or Loyalist troops. He left some 1,500 at Camden, sent Colonel Tarleton to chase Morgan and, with the rest of his army, moved to get between Greene and Morgan.

Now General Daniel Morgan was quite a different adversary than Lieutenant Colonel Banastre Tarleton had ever before encountered. And Morgan brought to this, his final battle, a tremendous amount of practical experience gained primarily in the school of hard knocks. His first military adventure had been as a teamster with Braddock's expedition. While so engaged he had gotten into an argument with a British officer and had proceeded to knock the man down. As punishment he was sentenced to receive several hundred lashes. That he was able to endure so many without losing consciousness is a little difficult to believe, but he certainly carried the scars of the beating to his grave. Nor did this experience deter him from taking an active part in the Virginia militia during the French and Indian War. Later he was commissioned a captain by the State of Virginia and participated in other expeditions against the Indians. There could have been very little he did not know about frontier warfare and he was an expert with the rifle and the tomahawk.

During this period he had also settled down, acquired some land and, although he had never received any formal schooling, he had painstakingly taught himself to read and write. Thus, by the beginning of the Revolution, he had become something of a leader in the Blue Ridge country of Virginia.

When the Continental Congress decided to authorize the formation of a Continental Army by raising ten companies of expert riflemen, Daniel Morgan was an obvious choice to command one of the two companies from Virginia. Upon arrival at the Siege of Boston, his was one of the three rifle companies selected to go with Benedict Arnold on the long, difficult march through the Maine woods to Quebec. Colonel Arnold obviously recognized Morgan's sterling qualities of leadership by placing him in command of the three rifle companies that led the way. At the ill-fated assault on Quebec, when General Montgomery was killed and Colonel Arnold wounded, Captain Morgan continued to fight, standing alone with his back against a wall, daring his enemies to shoot him. Even then he refused to give up his sword to a British "scoundrel," but handed it to an astonished clergyman who happened to be near.

After several months in prison, Morgan was exchanged and soon thereafter was commissioned a colonel to raise and command a corps of expert riflemen. When General Howe began his rather vague campaign in New Jersey in the late spring of 1777, Colonel Morgan's troops took an active part, but Washington soon decided that he and his riflemen could be far more useful elsewhere. Burgoyne was making slow but steady progress southward. If he was to be stopped, more Continental soldiers must be furnished to the northern department. Among those selected to be sent northward, Morgan's corps seemed particularly suitable for the task because they could take care of the marauding Indians who were prowling the woods in front of Burgoyne's army. The outstanding role played by Morgan and his men in the Battles of Freeman's Farm and Bemis Heights has already been described.

After Burgoyne's surrender at Saratoga, General Gates reluctantly returned Morgan's troops to Washington. Then, after the Valley Forge winter, his riflemen took part in the Monmouth Campaign, annoying and harassing Clinton on his march toward New York. After that his famous corps of experts was broken up and sent by companies for service against the Indians; some of them went with Sullivan's punitive expedition. Daniel Morgan soon found himself relegated to the command of an infantry regiment and suffered a bitter disappointment when Anthony Wayne was appointed to command the specially selected light infantry which took Stony Point.

Morgan's years of active campaigning and especially the strain he had undergone during the severe campaign through the forests to Quebec, followed by his imprisonment and the rigors of the Saratoga Campaign and Valley Forge, had told even on his iron constitution. Having been passed over for promotion, he took the opportunity to take a much-needed furlough. However, after the catastrophe at Camden, even though suffering acutely from ague and rheumatism, Morgan responded to the call of duty and at last found himself a brigadier general in command of an independent corps.

Warned of Tarleton's advance, General Morgan started to retreat, but not very far or very fast. He seemed to have become irritated at the necessity and was only looking for a good place to stand and fight. His choice of a battlefield has been greatly criticized by many authorities. It was at a place called the Cowpens, well known to the local people as a good area to round up their stray cattle, a wide, slightly hilly plain, with a few trees and very little underbrush. In other words, it was an excellent place for cavalry to operate—and Tarleton's dragoons heavily outnumbered Morgan's few available horse soldiers. Furthermore, the area was so wide that Morgan's flanks were completely open and the Broad River was at his back, just five miles away. Therefore, if he were defeated, there would be no chance of a successful retreat.

Both armies were about the same size, about 1,100 men each, but in trained regulars Tarleton outnumbered Morgan over two to one. It would seem, therefore, that Daniel Morgan was taking a terrible chance to hazard a battle under such conditions. Certainly, by now, he, of all people, knew how much more reliable his Continentals were than his militia. Half of his infantry were untrained, and many of these were armed with rifles and therefore could not possibly stand up to a British bayonet charge if it were pressed home.

General Morgan's preparations for the forthcoming battle were unique. First, he was resolved not to repeat the mistake Gates had made at Camden of placing his militia and his regulars in line together, inviting disaster for his trained men who would stand and fight after the militia on their flanks had fled. He could not do what Arnold had done so successfully in the battles preceding Saratoga, that is, put a couple of militia units between his veteran troops to be encouraged by their presence and steadiness in combat, because he had too many militia and too few trained troops. He would have to find some other solution.

General Morgan's Battle of Cowpens has been frequently compared with Hannibal's victory at Cannae, but his preparations for combat much more closely resemble the defense in depth which became standard practice in the final battles of World War I. He formed his men in three lines with his cavalry in reserve. The purpose of the first two lines was to disorganize the enemy attack, while the third line, composed of his most reliable soldiers, was to stop the enemy's final charge.

It may truthfully be said that Daniel Morgan's plan of battle was the culmination of all his years of experience, beginning with his younger days as a rifleman on the frontier, up to and including his personal observations of battle at Freeman's Farm and Bemis Heights, plus a careful study of the character and reputation of his adversary, Colonel Banastre Tarleton.

The latter was a very aggressive leader, disdainful of all Americans, entirely certain of victory, who could be expected to charge straight into battle, riding roughshod over all opposition, unprepared for anything unusual. He would probably rush headlong into the fray, not realizing until too late that he had stumbled into a trap. This was just what Morgan hoped he would do, and prepared his plans accordingly.

In his first line, Morgan decided to put 150 selected Georgia and North Carolina riflemen. These were placed about 150 yards in front of the second line. Naturally he did not expect them to stop the British-Loyalist troops, but they were all good shots. They were to hide behind trees, fire two rounds apiece, and then fall back into the second line which consisted of 300 North and South Carolina militia commanded by the famous partisan, Colonel Andrew Pickens. The two combined lines were to repeat the procedure, picking off as many of the enemy as they could before they also were to retire.

The third line, composed of his best troops, was to be 150 yards behind the second line. They were posted on a low hill, up whose slope the enemy would have to charge. General Morgan did not make the mistake of telling his combined first and second lines to fall back into his third. This would simply have caused confusion and disorganization. Colonel Pickens was to lead them around the left flank, thus clearing the field of fire.

This third line was under the command of Lieutenant Colonel John Eager Howard, a superb officer, and consisted of 320 of those excellent Maryland and Delaware Continentals, plus some Virginia and Georgia militia, most of whom had seen previous service in the Continental Army. This line had about 450 men in it and was the one on which Morgan was counting to win his battle.

The cavalry in reserve, to be used as the occasion demanded, was kept hidden behind a second smaller hill. It consisted of Lieutenant Colonel William Washington's 80 dragoons and 45 mounted infantry from Georgia.

Now Daniel Morgan was not the man simply to issue orders for a battle and then wait for them to be carried out, even by the most capable of officers. Long ago he had learned that the American soldier was an individualist who could follow orders but would do much better if he understood the reasons why they were issued. Particularly was this true of individuals who had not been inculcated with the strict discipline required of his veteran troops. Therefore, during a large part of the evening, and again in the early dawn before the battle, he went from campfire to campfire explaining his plan, not only to the officers in charge, but also to every man to whom he was able to talk. And, of all the great leaders of the American Revolution, Daniel Morgan, brought up on the frontier himself, was better able to talk to the men of his command in their own language than any other. A great number were frontiersmen themselves and the part that they would have to play was unusual to say the least. Joking, patting them on the back and encouraging them, he was able to infuse into his command the strong belief that his novel plan had every chance of success, and that the infamous Tarleton would be thoroughly defeated in the forthcoming battle.

Completely ignorant of Morgan's plans, but entirely certain of success, Colonel Tarleton awoke his men long before daybreak and sent them forward on a grueling night march in order to try to surprise his enemy. About dawn, January 17, 1781, scattered shots from American scouts warned the British colonel that he was approaching his enemy's position. Although his men were tired from their eight-mile march through swamps, on muddy roads, over unfamiliar broken ground, Tarleton immediately formed his infantry in line of battle. With 1,100 men, all but 100 of them well-trained British or Loyalist soldiers, Tarleton fully expected to drive the Americans in headlong flight to the north.

Riding forward to inspect the American position, Tarleton saw only the first or possibly the second line of Americans. Swiftly he sent his British Legion cavalry forward to disperse them. The Georgia and North Carolina riflemen, firing from behind the trees, calmly following the orders of their commander, inflicted so much damage upon Tarleton's British Legion cavalry that it quickly lost all interest in the battle

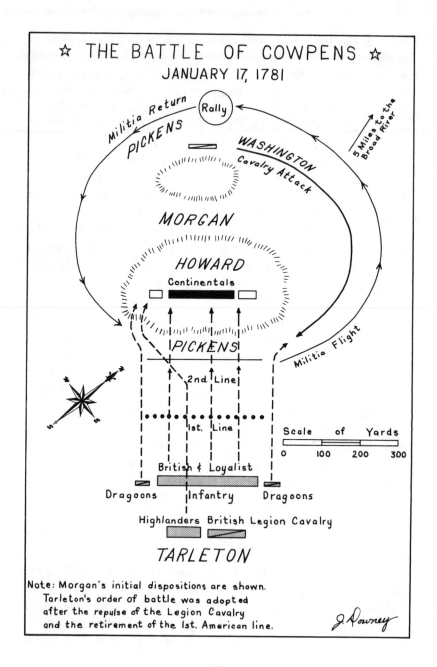

THE BATTLE OF COWPENS
JANUARY 17, 1781

Militia Return

Rally

PICKENS

WASHINGTON
Cavalry Attack

5 Miles to the Broad River

MORGAN

HOWARD

Continentals

PICKENS

2nd. Line

Militia Flight

1st. Line

Scale   of   Yards

0   100   200   300

British & Loyalist

Dragoons   Infantry   Dragoons

Highlanders   British Legion Cavalry

TARLETON

Note: Morgan's initial dispositions are shown.
Tarleton's order of battle was adopted
after the repulse of the Legion Cavalry
and the retirement of the 1st. American line.

J. Downey

and disappeared behind its own infantry. The American first line moved back to join the second American line.

Infuriated by this repulse, Colonel Tarleton did exactly what General Morgan had hoped he would do. Without any attempt to maneuver or outflank the American position, the British colonel launched an attack directly against the second American line. Tarleton's formation was straight out of the book, infantry in the center, some dragoons on each flank, with a Highland regiment in reserve together with the unhappy Legion cavalry. He was sure that the American second line would break and run, but he did not have the slightest notion that there was anything at all behind that second line. No doubt he knew that there were some Continental troops somewhere, but he probably supposed they were in the second line. These could be expected to hold in place while the militia fled, and then be overwhelmed as they had been at Camden.

From that moment onward it was entirely Daniel Morgan's battle; the impetuous Tarleton simply danced to Morgan's tune as he called every step. As directed, Colonel Andrew Pickens' South Carolina and North Carolina militia, encouraged by Morgan who was close behind them, fired their two volleys and then ran rapidly around to their left. The British infantry, seeing this apparently panic-stricken flight from the field, surged rapidly forward, certain that the victory was now theirs. In their eagerness some broke ranks. Therefore, when they were struck by the volley fire of Colonel Howard's third line, the effect was shocking even to the well-trained, disciplined British regulars.

Meanwhile, some of the dragoons on Tarleton's right flank, while attempting to pursue Pickens' men off the field, had been caught by another of Morgan's carefully conceived ideas. Colonel William Washington's cavalry had emerged from their hiding place behind the second hill and were chasing the dragoons off the field.

Having lost almost complete control of the battle, Colonel

Tarleton made a desperate effort to retrieve the situation. The men in his front line were courageously struggling uphill against Howard's steadfast line but suffering more casualties than the Americans. Even the two British artillery guns were having little effect upon the determined defenders. Banastre Tarleton had one resource left, the Highland regiment in reserve. If he could have foreseen the events of the next succeeding hour, the British commander could have used this fine regiment to cover the retreat of his already defeated army, but he could not bring himself to admit that he was being beaten by the Americans he despised so greatly. Therefore he sent the Highlanders to the left to outflank the right of the American third line.

Colonel John Howard ordered that end of his line to move backward at an angle to face the new attack. Through a misunderstanding, in the midst of the roar of combat, the whole third line thought a withdrawal had been ordered, which they began to execute calmly and in good order like the proud veterans they were.

Just at that crucial moment General Morgan appeared. He and Colonel Pickens had succeeded in re-forming the militia, out of sight behind the second hill. Now, under the leadership of Pickens, the militia were starting around the other side of the American line to have another try at the British, which was something that no one had ever really expected to occur.

Then everything happened so fast that none of the officers or soldiers of the opposing army ever recovered from the shock. Selecting another position for the retreating Continental line, Morgan told them, when they reached it, to turn about and fire a volley. Coming over the top of the hill in a rush, the British came within 50 yards of the Continentals when suddenly Colonel Howard's voice rang out. As one man, the American line swung about smartly, fired a precise volley from the hip, and, with bayonets fixed, charged straight forward. Completely unprepared, the British and Loyalist troops fell back, only to be hit again by Pickens' militia coming in on their left flank and by a simultaneous charge from Washington's cavalry, which had seized that moment to strike them on their right flank.

Surprised and crushed by the smashing force of the unexpected bayonet charge from the front, enveloped on both flanks by the militia and the cavalry, most of Tarleton's troops had no choice but to surrender. Though they had fought a good battle, the unsuspecting British-Loyalist soldiers had been led into a trap from which there was no possible escape. Only the Highlanders continued to resist until they too were overwhelmed, while the artillerymen, true to the tradition of their service, died defending their guns to the last. Very, very few of the British force which had advanced so confidently to battle that day escaped. Several of the horsemen of Tarleton's Loyalist British Legion got away, as did Colonel Tarleton himself, but his ruthless arrogance had received a fearful blow, from which it never recovered.

Daniel Morgan's victory was so complete that the figures are still hard to believe. The American loss in the Battle of Cowpens was only 12 killed and 60 wounded. The British and Loyalists had over 100 killed, and over 800 captured, of whom 229 were wounded. At a single stroke nearly one-third of Lord Cornwallis' field army had been wiped out. It takes very little imagination to picture the delight and joy with which the story of this victory was received throughout the country. Many at first may have doubted the surprising news until it was confirmed, but that it had happened to the hated Tarleton at the hands of Daniel Morgan made the news doubly welcome.

Before the next moves in this campaign in the Carolinas are described, it would be well to analyze this battle, which was certainly one of the most perfectly fought, classic victories in military history. First, Morgan had at last found, and demonstrated, a way to use militia in a battle. This was something that had baffled the best, and the worst, American generals since the beginning of the Revolution. During the British retreat from Concord, the minutemen had inflicted numerous casualties by sniping at the retreating redcoats from the sides of the road. At Bunker Hill, militia had bravely withstood attack when protected by entrenchments, but from that point onward they had proved almost worthless to Washington in all his battles. In fact, the Father of our Country had grown to distrust them completely.

John Stark's victory at Bennington, when the militia had outnumbered their opponents overwhelmingly, has already been described, as has Arnold's limited use of two regiments at Saratoga. The Battle of King's Mountain had been a very special case of untrained militia versus untrained militia.

It had been left to General Daniel Morgan to find a real solution to the problem. For some reason, which cannot stand careful analysis, it has become popular to describe Morgan as a simple backwoodsman whose experience was primarily limited to guerrilla fighting. In actuality, he was, by the time Cowpens was fought, one of the most capable professional soldiers in the American Continental Army. If he had been as ignorant or as thoughtless as Gates, he might very probably have repeated the latter's mistake at Camden. The inescapable truth, however, is that Morgan pinned almost all his hopes of success on his tried and trusted Continentals who would have to meet and turn back the British regulars' final charge.

The real explanation for the success of the militia at Cowpens was that Morgan did not expect them to do too much, and carefully explained exactly what he hoped they would be able to accomplish. Thus, they were not demoralized, but felt pleased that they had been able to perform their somewhat limited mission successfully. If they had fled in defeat, they could never have been rallied and brought back around to the other side of the American line to aid in the final British defeat. Furthermore, their initial contribution to the victory had not been solely the killing or wounding of some of the advancing enemy. Their pretended flight had led Tarleton and his men to assume that this was to be another simple, easy victory. The result was an exaggerated feeling of shock when they encountered the steadfast Continentals standing firmly as a rock. Whether such surprise tactics would work as well again remained to be seen, on another field on another day.

Because of the fact that Cowpens ended in a double envelopment by the militia on one flank and the cavalry on the other, many people have come to regard it as another Cannae on a smaller scale. That Morgan, unlike Hannibal at the beginning of his battle, had no such intention is obvious, not only from his dispositions but also from his explanations to his men. They were formed in a series of lines of increasing strength. Even in the third line, the best troops, the Maryland and Delaware Continentals, were placed in the center. There was no suggestion whatever of the center retreating while the wings closed in to effect the classic double envelopment of Cannae. That the militia returned to attack the British flank was as much a pleasant surprise to Morgan as to anyone else on the American side.

Although nearly one-third of Cornwallis' field army had been eliminated, the remainder was yet more powerful than Greene's and Morgan's combined strength. Furthermore, the two American armies were separated by a distance of nearly 140 miles. There was every chance that Cornwallis might get between them and destroy each in turn, recapturing the hundreds of prisoners taken by Morgan. The events of the next two months form an exciting chapter in the history of the United States, but it is not properly Daniel Morgan's story. He had done more than his share to set the stage, but the strenuous physical efforts he had forced himself to make had been too much for his ailing body to endure. Suffering so acutely from the aches and pains of rheumatism that he could no longer even ride a horse, Morgan stayed to supervise the escape of his army with his prisoners, then was forced to retire from active duty in the field, leaving as his monument and his gift to his country, one of the most superbly fought, decisive battles in American history.

9

Lord Cornwallis
Chases an Elusive Foe

Of the four British generals who commanded armies that fought on the soil of the thirteen colonies for long periods of time, and whose names are therefore best known to Americans, two emerged from the war with sufficient military reputation to continue their careers as soldiers. The American Revolution was the graveyard for the hopes of the other two.

The first to return home to England was "Gentleman Johnny" Burgoyne. For his failures, leading to the surrender at Saratoga, he was denounced in the House of Commons and deprived of his offices, retaining only his military rank. Thus, his career as a soldier was abruptly finished and, in his case, the judgment of his contemporaries seems appropriate, though somewhat harsh, in view of the fact that Lord George Germain, the completely incompetent civilian cabinet minister in charge of colonial affairs, had contributed so generously toward the failure of the British strategic plan. But then Burgoyne had gone ahead to prove his unfitness for the command assigned to him by repeating again and again the same mistakes, ignoring or neglecting basic military principles, until he had led his army to disaster.

Sir William Howe's treatment upon his return to England was far different. He and his brother, Admiral Lord Richard Howe, became engaged in an unpleasant controversy with the government, but the reputation of neither was greatly damaged, and both continued to serve their country well in positions of great responsibility. Admiral Howe became particularly famous in British naval history for his part in the final relief of the Siege of Gibraltar in 1782 and for his victory in 1794 over a French fleet in the great naval battle fought over 400 miles from the mainland, henceforth known as the "Battle of the Glorious First of June."

The other two British generals who became so well known in American history were, of course, Sir Henry Clinton and Lieutenant General Lord Charles Cornwallis. For months the two had been advocating to their home government completely different policies for the conduct of the war, and each saw in the events that had just occurred complete justification of his own viewpoint. General Clinton, the commander of the British Army in North America, with headquarters in New York, had no intention of conducting a large-scale campaign in the north and had been completely satisfied with the war in the south, the capture of Charleston, the victory at Camden, and the subjugation of Georgia and South Carolina. The Battle of King's Mountain had been, in his opinion, exactly the sort of thing that could have been expected when unnecessary risks were taken. He had said again and again that extensive operations into the interior of the country were hazardous and unnecessary, when time was on the side of the British. During the fall of the year 1780, Sir Henry felt, and historians have certainly agreed with him, that the colonial cause had reached a very low point indeed. Given just a little more time, Clinton believed that the war-weary colonists, faced with financial ruin, would gradually succumb. Resistance in North Carolina and Virginia would then, each in turn, collapse and the remainder of the colonies would follow suit.

In his planning, Sir Henry had certainly not overlooked Virginia; the city of Portsmouth had been the target for one of his devastating raids which were calculated to undermine the American will to resist. And just before the Battle of Cowpens, he had sent a British force led by Benedict Arnold, now a brigadier in the British Army, into Virginia. It had sailed partway up the James River, landed and marched into

Richmond, destroyed a great deal of property, and then encamped for the remainder of the winter at Portsmouth. As far as General Clinton was concerned, the war was going well, though slowly, except for those unfortunate expeditions that his subordinate, Lord Cornwallis, was forever sending into the interior of the country. Any defeats suffered by them would unnecessarily encourage the colonists and thus prolong the war. When the news of the Battle of Cowpens reached him, it only served to increase his apprehensions, but he had no chance to influence General Cornwallis who had already taken action in accordance with his own ideas as to the way the war should be fought.

Cornwallis was cut from an entirely different bolt of cloth than his superior officer and it is an interesting commentary upon human nature that their receptions upon their return to England were completely dissimilar. Whether or not Sir Henry Clinton's methods could have been successful in the long run (and it is very questionable that they would have been), the slow, cautious approach is seldom appreciated by the general public, whereas all the world loves a fighter, especially one who comes very close to winning.

The year the Revolution ended Clinton published his narrative of the campaign. It immediately provoked a response from Cornwallis, with whom almost everyone promptly sided. Whereas Sir Henry spent the rest of his life trying to defend his actions, the general who actually surrendered at Yorktown was met with sympathy and a feeling that if he had been in overall command the outcome of the war could have been vastly different. After Yorktown, Lord Cornwallis was appointed governor general of India, where he greatly furthered British interests. Later he served with distinction as viceroy of Ireland, and then was sent back to India, where he died in the year 1805.

It is easy to understand why Cornwallis was popular with the King, his ministers, and the people. Lord Cornwallis' record, prior to the Revolution, had been excellent. In the American war, where others had appeared slow to act, Cornwallis had demonstrated energy, courage, and resolution. Though he had sailed with the troops on the expedition to Charleston in 1776, none of the blame for that naval fiasco had become attached to him. At the Battle of Long Island he had exhibited initiative and vigor. Then, in the capture of Fort Washington, the troops under Cornwallis' command had done so well that General Howe had given him the task of capturing Fort Lee across the Hudson River. This assignment, also, was accomplished rapidly and with such ease that General Nathanael Greene and his entire command were almost captured in the process. Thereupon Cornwallis had begun a vigorous pursuit across New Jersey. Later, when General Howe decided that the campaign was ended and the war won, for all practical purposes, Cornwallis asked for and received permission to return to England on leave.

Then came the stunning news of Washington's counterattack at Trenton. Cornwallis' home leave was abruptly canceled; he was sent posthaste to take command in New Jersey. On the evening of January 2, 1777, he thought he had successfully trapped Washington's army south of Trenton, with its back to the Delaware River, in a position from which there could be no escape. A concentrated British attack in the fading darkness of that winter evening would probably have met with success, but Cornwallis decided to wait until the next day. The "old fox was safe." He could "bag him in the morning."

In the morning came the guns of Princeton, behind Cornwallis' lines. Exhorting his troops to march at maximum speed, driving them onward across the freezing, icy stream beside the Princeton battlefield, Cornwallis arrived just in time to see the rear guard of the American army moving out of the town. It was a bitter lesson for the aggressive Lord Cornwallis, one he would never forget. From that time forward this British general would never again be criticized for lack of energy. If anything, he would henceforth be labeled overly aggressive.

The outstanding part played by Cornwallis in the flank attack at the Battle of the Brandywine has already been told, as has his stunning victory at the Battle of Camden. Now in January, 1781, he was again faced by Nathanael Greene, whom he had almost made prisoner over four years before at Fort Lee. His trusted British cavalry lieutenant, Banastre Tarleton, had just suffered overwhelming defeat at the Battle of Cowpens. This repulse suffered by British arms must be quickly avenged, and the impression created in the public mind reversed, or incalculable harm would result. More of the rebellious colonists would feel renewed hope in their cause; that unfortunate affair at King's Mountain the preceding October had been bad enough. There, no British troops had been involved, but at Cowpens the British Army itself had been badly defeated. Immediate action of the most positive sort was required.

There was no doubt whatever in Cornwallis' mind as to what course to pursue. He reported the news of Cowpens to Clinton in New York. Then, before his superior could make any effort to stop him, he committed his troops to a course of action which he knew would never be approved by his more cautious commander in New York.

It is easy to follow Cornwallis' reasoning. After the repulse of the combined American-French effort to retake Savannah, resistance in Georgia had ceased. The capture of the first part of the Continental Army at the Siege of Charleston, followed by the overwhelming defeat of the second part at Camden, had resulted in the collapse of all organized resistance in South Carolina. The partisans who had fled to the swamps had been irritating during this period, but their efforts had not been much more than a source of annoyance. They were a terribly stubborn lot and never seemed to know when to quit. As long as the British won victories, these partisans would gain few adherents. When, eventually, their leaders were killed, they would lose heart and resistance would certainly die out. This had been Cornwallis' reasoning until the

Battle of King's Mountain had caused a sudden increase in the number of partisans. Now the news of Cowpens would cause even more followers to join the original groups.

It was obvious to Cornwallis that news of American victories would always result in an increase in partisan activity. In like manner, a swift British victory would have the opposite effect. Another battle like Camden was badly needed. If this could be achieved the effect would be twofold. Most of the recent followers of the partisan leaders would again return to their homes and, of far greater importance, the southern Continental army might cease to exist. The enemy could never survive another British victory like Camden. Organized resistance in North Carolina would then collapse; Cornwallis could invade Virginia and, once firmly established in that important colony, he could look forward with confidence to the end of the American Revolution.

It might seem strange that Lord Cornwallis could think in such positive terms of victory so soon after the stunning defeat of his lieutenant at Cowpens, but there were excellent reasons. He still had about 3,000 men, most of whom were good, reliable soldiers. His enemy's strength was not known with any degree of accuracy, but Cornwallis felt sure that he outnumbered his opponents in trained soldiers and, furthermore, he knew his enemy's forces were widely separated. The British had only to move forward, get between the two little American armies, and destroy them both in turn. It was not even hard to determine which one to strike at first. Morgan had just fought a battle; his men would be tired; there would be wounded to care for; and Morgan's retreat would be slowed by the hundreds of prisoners whom Cornwallis was most anxious to recover.

In his calculations, the British leader made one mistake. He assumed that Morgan, after his great victory of January 17, would take a little time to rest his men, make preparations for his retreat, and organize his march column. Cornwallis therefore aimed his pursuit to intercept Morgan only a short distance in the rear of the Cowpens battlefield. By so doing, he entirely miscalculated Morgan's capacity for rapid, decisive action. Within two hours after the end of the battle, the first of Morgan's men were already on the move. The prisoners were sent by a different, more protected route and, by keeping his troops moving at a rapid pace, Morgan evaded Cornwallis' first effort to cut off his retreat.

Initially his American opponent, Nathanael Greene, had been so heavily outnumbered that he had been completely unable to plan any operations that might involve a pitched battle with Cornwallis' army. Therefore, Greene had divided his forces to act in the manner of the partisans, on a larger scale than they were capable of doing. Now, the wiping out of nearly one-third of Cornwallis' army at Cowpens permitted General Greene to entertain ideas that had previously been far beyond his capabilities with the troops available; dim hopes of a brighter future began to flicker on the horizon. Counting both his own and Morgan's men, Greene could muster nearly 1,300 Continentals and perhaps 1,500 militia. His 1,300 could not engage Cornwallis' 3,000 with any hope of success, no matter how many militia came to the scene, but the odds were a lot better than before. Eventually some of the Continentals, now being trained in Virginia, might arrive. Then, perhaps, using the militia as Morgan had done, the decision might be entrusted to the god of battles.

In the meantime, however, Greene's two little armies were in a perilous position, widely separated, retreating as rapidly as possible to avoid destruction. At this moment General Greene had no choice but to retreat. In the process, great numbers of the militia would certainly drift homeward, but the pursuers would lose men also. Nearer the Virginia border, with more Continentals closer by, the numbers might become more nearly equal.

Because Morgan had gotten past him, Cornwallis could have concluded that his best chance to catch and destroy his enemies one by one had gone. He could have halted his pursuit and few would have blamed him for doing so, certainly not his cautious superior, Sir Henry Clinton, in New York. But this was not Cornwallis' way. He was determined to engage the American army in battle. If the two parts could not be defeated in turn in two separate battles, he was perfectly ready, willing, and able, with his superior numbers, to fight Greene wherever he might catch him. King's Mountain and Cowpens must be avenged.

Cornwallis' next move was unusual, and somewhat reminiscent of Cortez' destruction of his ships before invading the interior of Mexico. All excess supplies, spare tentage, and extra wagons were burned. Only the bare necessities remained. Without extra wagons to transport additional supplies, the men would have to make long strenuous marches with only the food and clothing they could carry on their backs; but with only a small wagon train the army could move much more rapidly. This gesture on Lord Cornwallis' part was partly psychological. His soldiers would be impressed with the urgency of making every effort to catch the fleeing Americans. Anyone who has ever served in an army can imagine their feelings when they saw their almost irreplaceable belongings committed to the flames, their precious rum ration poured onto the ground, even the commanding general's belongings going up in smoke. There could be no doubt in their minds that their commander was committed irrevocably to catching the Americans if it were humanly possible.

The race was on, and upon its outcome the fate of the south rested. There was no doubt whatever in Nathanael Greene's mind that his enemy would conduct a ruthless pursuit, bending every effort, night and day, to catch his little army. If Cornwallis won, and the Americans were caught, it would mean the end of the little army entrusted to his care. The Carolinas would be British, and possibly Virginia also. If Greene escaped, the British would eventually be forced to turn back. Then a stronger American army might return to do battle, and the south might yet be torn from British hands. Neither side could afford to lose the race; too much depended upon its outcome.

The story of Washington's retreat, in 1776, across New Jersey, ending in the dramatic American victories of Trenton and Princeton, is well known to every schoolchild, but the retreat across North Carolina into Virginia deserves greater prominence than is usually accorded to it in our history books. Although the distances involved in the 1781 retreat were greater, the time consumed was less because both armies moved more rapidly. The privations endured and the results of the battles that followed were, in the long run, comparable.

On January 28, after the destruction of his army's baggage, Lord Cornwallis set his troops in motion to pursue Morgan as rapidly as possible. His opponent, General Greene, had already guessed that Morgan's army would continue to be Cornwallis' first objective and, on that same day, was riding across country to the point of greatest danger, leaving the rest of his army to march northward under the command of Brigadier General Isaac Huger. On February 6, at Guilford Court House, Greene, with Morgan's column, met Huger and the reunited army marched northward toward Virginia.

Nathanael Greene now organized a corps of light troops to act as rear guard, to slow the British advance, break down bridges, harass the enemy, and protect the main column from attack by the pursuers. Because General Morgan was now suffering such acute pain from ague and rheumatism that he could no longer continue active service with the army, Greene entrusted the command of this corps to Colonel Otho H. Williams, the officer who had rendered such outstanding service on the battlefield of Camden while in temporary command of the reserve brigade of Maryland Continentals. In this new assignment Colonel Williams fully justified Greene's confidence.

The weather was miserable, rainy and cold; the roads were

clogged with sticky, red-clay mud which, when not slippery, froze into deep hard ruts. The Americans were poorly equipped and badly clothed in tattered rags and worn shoes, or walking barefoot. The pursuing British, led by Brigadier General Charles O'Hara, on several occasions came close enough to be within musket range, but never once did Colonel Williams or his light corps fail in their assigned mission of preventing the pursuers from attacking the main column. In the performance of this duty, Williams and his men were aided by the fact that they were often able to use boats to cross rivers and streams, while the pursuers had to wade through the freezing waters. The sufferings endured by the British on these occasions in such bitterly cold water tended, in part, to counterbalance their better clothing and equipment. To add to the miseries of both sides, the rain at times alternated with snow; yet both pursuers and pursued marched forward with determination, setting a heartbreaking pace. At times it must have seemed to each side that they were being asked to exceed the powers of human endurance, but both knew the value of the great prize that hung in the balance.

At the very beginning of the race, General Greene had fixed upon the River Dan in southern Virginia as his ultimate objective. If he could reach and cross that obstacle, his army would be close enough to reinforcements so that he could consider his men safe. Cornwallis also fully recognized the importance of the Dan River. If he could not catch Greene and bring him to battle south of that line, the British would have to retreat. They would be too far from their supply bases and would be forced to return empty-handed.

In wintertime the waters of the Dan were too high to be crossed at the lower fords without boats. Therefore, when Lord Cornwallis found that Colonel Williams' rearguard corps was marching toward the upper fords, he leaped to the conclusion that sufficient boats had not been found, that the whole American army was going to cross upstream, and strove to reach the upper fords before the Americans. At this point the race became an hour-by-hour venture, with pursuers and pursued in almost constant contact, each halting only long enough for a very short rest at night and one hasty meal a day.

Cornwallis did not know that in these last stages he was following only the light corps. Nathanael Greene had long before sent back word to gather boats at the lower fords. These had been collected in advance, but there were not enough for the whole army to cross simultaneously. Therefore, Colonel Williams had been given the additional mission of luring Cornwallis' troops westward, while the main army crossed at the lower fords. Greene's baggage and supplies were ferried across, then the main army, but Williams' men were still in grave danger of being sacrificed. At last, the light corps swerved sharply to the northeast, hoping that their efforts, and extra marching in a false direction, had given Greene time to get across, and return the boats for them to use. Until the last moment, the men could not be sure that their commander's timing had been accurate. To protect the crossing of the main army, they still might have to turn and give battle against far greater numbers.

It was the afternoon of February 14, 1781, when, still many weary miles from the river, word came from Greene that the main army was safe and the boats were waiting for them. The worn, tired men raised a cheer and pressed onward. General O'Hara's British troops were so close that they heard those cheers. Uncertain of the significance, but knowing that this was their last chance to catch the enemy they had pursued for so many weary days, British officers urged their men to redouble their efforts. But, with the winning of the race almost in sight, Colonel Williams' men would not stop now to rest or lag behind. The last of the Americans reached the Dan River long after dark had fallen, but by midnight, when General O'Hara's men came to the water's edge, the boats were gone.

When Lord Cornwallis heard the news he knew that he

would now have to turn back. Many would congratulate him on the speed with which he had chased the American army out of North Carolina up into Virginia. On the surface it might appear that his pursuit had been very successful, but he had wanted to destroy Greene's army, not simply chase it away. A victory in battle had been his prime objective, but he had failed to achieve this basic goal and knew very well that his opponents would return again. Some historians have criticized him for taking two days at the beginning of his pursuit to burn all his baggage, but if it had been left behind with an inadequate guard, it would probably have fallen into the hands of the American militia. Cornwallis did not want to leave a large body of troops with his baggage because his prime objective was to completely crush the Americans in battle; for this he wanted every available soldier present. Therefore, he decided to burn his wagons because, with a long supply train, his army could never have marched at the furious, sustained rate it achieved, often as much as thirty miles a day, which is hard to imagine under the terrible road and weather conditions that prevailed. The remarkable fortitude, endurance, and devotion to duty exhibited by his soldiers had been in the best tradition of the British Army, but these qualities had been matched by Greene's Americans who, on their final day, had actually marched forty miles in sixteen hours to reach the Dan River.

It is, admittedly, not normal to praise a successful retreat but the results that flowed from the famous retreat to the Dan were indeed unusual and far-reaching. Cornwallis was forced to turn back but refused to withdraw farther than Hillsboro, North Carolina, where he attempted to save face by announcing that the state was now under British control and inviting the Loyalists to come fight with him against the rebels. Very few people were convinced by this proclamation. It was all too evident that the issue had not yet been decided. Half-hearted, timid Loyalists could not be attracted by such a dubious prospect, and there were not many devout Tories in this part of North Carolina.

During the last days of February and the early part of March, the Americans were very annoying to Cornwallis. They conducted little raiding expeditions, constantly changed their positions, apparently offered battle, but when he made an effort to attack them, again escaped. Therefore, when Lord Cornwallis learned on March 14 that Nathanael Greene had moved to Guilford Court House and was actually preparing to fight, he moved his army immediately toward the American position. Of course it was obvious to the British general that his enemy must have received reinforcements or he would not now be hazarding a battle. But Cornwallis was entirely ready to commit his troops to action, no matter what the odds. For two months he had been exerting every effort to force his foe to meet him in combat. Now that the Americans were willing to take their chances, Cornwallis was certainly ready to take his.

The battle that followed is not simple to describe and it is almost as difficult to reconcile the numbers involved. Lieutenant General Cornwallis had begun his pursuit to the Dan with about 3,000 men, most of them reliable British and Hessians, or trained Loyalists. The majority of the Tory militia, unwilling to sustain the rigors of the arduous winter campaign, had long since left for home and very few others had come to take their places. The losses among his trained soldiers due to death, wounds, and sickness, had amounted to about 250 men, which was comparable to the losses sustained by the American Continentals. Thus, Cornwallis should have had about 2,200 men to send into battle, but most historians contend that only about 1,900 were actually engaged at Guilford Court House. The difference is hard to explain. Some soldiers undoubtedly remained in camp to aid the British sick and wounded, or guard whatever supplies and wagons had been accumulated. However, it is difficult to believe that the same general who had burned his supplies in order to bring the maximum number of soldiers with him on a march would now leave behind as many as 300 men. Cornwallis was extremely anxious to meet the Americans in battle and moved early in the morning of March 15 toward Greene's position, without even allowing his men a chance to have breakfast. His principal concern seems to have been that if he gave the American general time to think about the coming battle, the Americans might not be there when he arrived.

The British leader need not have worried about General Nathanael Greene reversing his decision. Ever since the latter had taken command of the southern department he had been trying to create a situation where he could engage his British enemy on fairly equal terms. Even after Morgan's victory at Cowpens, General Greene had not been strong enough to risk a major battle. He had engineered the retreat to the Dan primarily for the purpose of equalizing the strength of the two armies. During the course of that memorable campaign his Continental infantry and cavalry had suffered approximately the same losses as those sustained by Cornwallis' veteran soldiers. The militia had largely disappeared, but now these men were beginning to return and some Continental reinforcements had at last arrived.

At the beginning of the retreat to the Dan the American army had consisted of nearly 1,300 Continentals and 1,500 militia. But the arrival of the Virginia Continentals more than offset the losses in trained troops sustained during the retreat. General Greene felt that this was as good an opportunity as he would ever have to defeat Cornwallis' army. He could not predict the future. There was no way of forecasting whether more militia would march to his aid, or when those now with him might choose to go home; he had better use them immediately while he had his hands on them. It was for that purpose that he had marched to Guilford Court House, a place he had previously selected on his retreat as a favorable location in which to fight a battle. He felt absolutely certain that, if he waited there, his aggressive opponent would rush to attack him in his chosen position.

As usual, Greene faced the problems that every American general always faced when he had to rely upon militia as a part of his army. How could they be most useful? To what extent could he rely upon them? Just two months before, General Daniel Morgan had demonstrated how militia could be utilized, and that they would respond enthusiastically if they were not asked to do too much. There is no doubt that Greene had talked at length with Morgan on the subject, knowing that some day he might have to fight a battle under conditions perhaps similar to those that prevailed at Cowpens. Also, Daniel Morgan, after returning to his home to try to recover his strength, had given a great deal of thought to the subject, and had written to Greene suggesting how the coming battle should be fought. Knowing of the existence of this letter, a number of people, recognizing the apparent similarity of Greene's dispositions on March 15, 1781, at Guilford Court House, have leaped to the conclusion that Greene was simply trying to copy Morgan's Cowpens victory. Such a conclusion is entirely unwarranted and gives little credit to either Greene or to Cornwallis. The latter must certainly have talked with Colonel Tarleton about the Cowpens disaster and learned exactly what had happened on that battlefield. Therefore, Nathanael Greene could not simply repeat Morgan's tactics; his opponent was far too experienced an officer to fall for exactly the same tricks that had defeated his overeager subordinate only two months before.

General Greene studied the composition of his forces. He had four Continental infantry regiments, two Legions, and a few artillerymen. The units known as Legions contained both infantry and cavalry. They were commanded by Lieutenant Colonel William Washington and Lieutenant Colonel Henry "Light Horse Harry" Lee, father of General Robert E. Lee and the author of the famous toast to Washington, "First in War, First in Peace, and First in the Hearts of his Countrymen."

Colonel Washington's Legion contained the élite Delaware light infantry company commanded by Captain Robert Kirkwood, who was undoubtedly the finest example on record of the devotion to duty shown by the officers of the Continental Army. In his *Memoirs of the War in the Southern Department,* Colonel Lee wrote:

> The State of Delaware furnished one regiment only; and certainly no regiment in the army surpassed it in soldiership. The remnant of that corps, less than two companies, from the battle of Camden, was commanded by Captain Kirkwood, who passed through the war with high reputation; and yet as the line of Delaware consisted but of one regiment, and that regiment was reduced to a captain's command, Kirkwood never could be promoted in regular routine—a very glaring defect in the organization of the army . . . . The sequel is singularly hard. Kirkwood retired, upon peace, a captain; and when the army under St. Clair was raised to defend the West from the Indian enemy, this veteran resumed his sword as the oldest captain of the oldest regiment.
>
> In the decisive defeat of the 4th of November, the gallant Kirkwood fell, bravely sustaining his point of the action. It was the thirty-third time he had risked his life for his country; and he died as he had lived, the brave, meritorious, unrewarded, Kirkwood.

The other Delaware company was serving as an integral part of the famous 1st Maryland. At that period of history, this regiment, composed of the old reliable Maryland and Delaware Continentals, was probably the finest fighting unit in the world. These men could be trusted implicitly and, in the final analysis, Greene's hopes for victory rested on the shoulders of these battle-hardened veterans.

The other three Continental regiments, the 5th Maryland and the 4th and 5th Virginia, had been but recently formed and were untried in combat. They had excellent officers to command them and some veterans in the ranks, but it was difficult to predict how well these units would meet the test on their first day of battle.

The personnel belonging to the Continental Army numbered approximately:

```
1,600 infantry, including those in the Legions
  160 cavalry
   60 artillery
————
1,820 Total
```

The militia contribution consisted of:

```
1,000 North Carolina militia
1,200 Virginia militia
  400 Virginia riflemen, in 2 units of 200 each
————
2,600 Total
```

The grand total of the American army was therefore 4,420 men. It was a most heterogeneous force, over one-third Continentals and less than two-thirds militia. This division of the troops almost into thirds undoubtedly was a contributing factor in Greene's decision to form his army into three lines, as Morgan had done at Cowpens. The lines were not, however, placed close together. General Greene could be certain that a really good, battle-wise leader of Cornwallis' caliber could not be induced, after Tarleton's disaster, to let his troops charge headlong from one line into another, shattering their formations as they did so. Cornwallis would certainly halt to regroup and reappraise the situation between lines. Therefore, because the terrain lent itself to a defense in greater depth, the American army was disposed in three lines with about 350 yards between the first two and a somewhat greater distance between the second and third.

Of course, the most important of the three lines was the third or final line. There, win, lose, or draw, the battle would be decided. Brigadier General Isaac Huger commanded the right half of the line composed of the 4th and 5th Virginia regiments. Colonel Otho Williams was in command of the left half where the 1st and 5th Maryland Continentals were formed.

In the second line General Greene put the Virginia militia because they were reported to be somewhat better trained than the North Carolina militia who were placed in the first line. The latter were, like the foremost lines at Cowpens, asked only to fire two rounds, then fall back.

Thus far, Greene's dispositions were practically an exact repetition of those of Morgan. However, there was one major difference. Nathanael Greene had implicit faith in the valor and steadiness of the veterans of the 1st Maryland, but since he could not be so certain of the other Continental regiments, he took measures calculated to lessen the shock of the final British assault upon that vital third line. Instead of placing Washington's and Lee's Legions in reserve, he put them in positions where they would be in continuous contact with the enemy from the beginning to the end of the battle. On each side of the first line, 200 of the Virginia riflemen were drawn up so that they could fire partially across the front of an advancing British force. At the extreme ends of each of these oblique lines, the Legions were placed, infantry in front, cavalry slightly behind. Greene could hope that not only would the presence of the veteran Legions on the flanks strengthen the first line, but as the Legions retired, their continued resistance would inflict greater casualties upon the enemy and thus lessen the power and shock effect of the bayonet charges on the succeeding lines.

In contrast to this mixed force, Cornwallis' army, though less than half their enemy's numerical strength, was composed entirely of veteran units. As soon as he reached the battlefield, the British general moved his troops into position

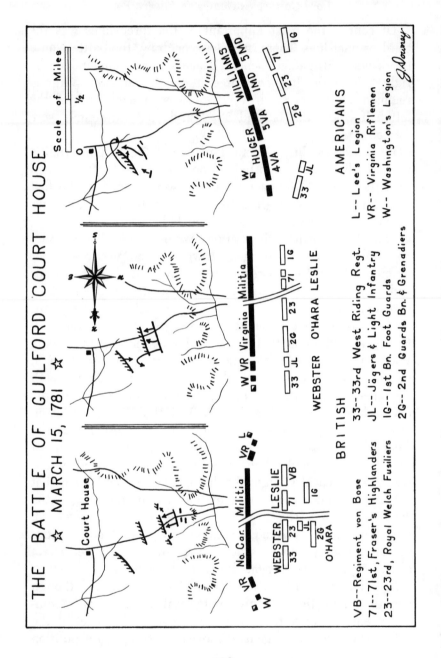

THE BATTLE OF GUILFORD COURT HOUSE
☆ MARCH 15, 1781 ☆

Scale of Miles

WILLIAMS 5MD
IMD
HUGER 5VA
4VA

1G
7I
23
2G
JL
33

Virginia Militia

WEBSTER O'HARA LESLIE

1G
7I
23
JL 2G
33

No. Car. Militia
LESLIE
WEBSTER
33 23 7I VB
JL 1G
2G
O'HARA

Court House

AMERICANS

L-- Lee's Legion
VR-- Virginia Riflemen
W-- Washington's Legion

BRITISH

VB--Regiment von Bose
71--71st, Fraser's Highlanders
23--23rd, Royal Welch Fusiliers
33--33rd West Riding Regt.
JL--Jägers & Light Infantry
1G--1st Bn. Foot Guards
2G--2nd Guards Bn. & Grenadiers

192

without pausing even to give his men time to get something to eat during this day of combat. Major General Alexander Leslie was placed in command of the right half of the line, south of the road, facing toward the east. His troops consisted of: the Regiment von Bose, one of the best of the Hessian units; the 71st or Fraser's Highlanders; and the 1st Battalion of the Royal Foot Guards in support. The commander of the left half of the British line, north of the road, was Lieutenant Colonel James Webster. Here were placed the 23rd, Royal Welch Fusiliers, and the 33rd, West Riding, Regiment. To their rear were the jägers, the light infantry, the grenadiers, and the 2nd Battalion of Foot Guards commanded by Brigadier General O'Hara. Tarleton's dragoons were held in reserve. The total strength, as previously noted, was only 1,900 men but shortly after one o'clock on the afternoon of March 15, 1781, the British and Hessians advanced confidently and proudly to the attack, expecting on this battlefield to put an end to the war in the south.

As the soldiers moved forward in precise straight lines, perpendicular to both sides of the road, the men found that they were marching eastward along a shallow valley. The area was dotted with trees but these were not numerous enough to restrict their movement. They could see through the leaves for a distance of about 300 yards. To their front and right and left the ground sloped gently upward but no enemy appeared on either side. The soldiers came upon two clearings in the woods; the troops advanced across them until suddenly greeted by a blast of fire from the rail fence on the far side. Though a few men fell, the lines continued steadily forward, ignoring the casualties, until halted at the word of command to deliver a volley of musketry at the defenders sheltered by the fence; then they charged with the bayonet. A second blast of gunfire caused the attackers to recoil for a moment but then, urged onward by their officers, the British and Hessians reached the rail fence to find it deserted. The North Carolina militia had done exactly what they had been asked to do: fire two rounds and then run from the field.

Before the attackers could begin to congratulate themselves for having so easily disposed of nearly one-fourth of the Americans, they found that they were being subjected to a deadly crossfire from both flanks. The bullets were coming from two groups of Americans on each side of them who continued to hold their ground even though almost all of the 1,000 militia posted at the rail fence in the center of their line had disappeared at a dead run. These men on the flanks were, of course, Washington's Legion, Lee's Legion, and the Virginia riflemen, plus one company of North Carolina militia which had not left the field.

In order to attack these two groups, posted at an angle to their line, the officers in command of the flank units hastily wheeled their troops to the right and left to drive these men also from the field. This task was not so easily accomplished. The 33rd, West Riding, Regiment supported by the jägers and the light infantry made only slow progress on the left. Here, the 200 Virginia riflemen, Kirkwood's light infantry, and Washington's cavalrymen withdrew through the trees, continuing to fire as they gave ground. The same sort of thing occurred on the right flank except that the retreating units on that side were gradually pushed away from the main battlefield toward the higher ground to the south. There developed in this sector an entirely separate battle involving primarily the Regiment von Bose, the infantry and cavalry of Lee's Legion, and the other 200 Virginia riflemen.

To maintain the momentum of the attack, General Leslie brought forward the 1st Battalion of Foot Guards. This unit helped shove Lee's Legion aside and then advanced in line with the Highlanders. On the left (north) side of the road, General O'Hara had also strengthened the British line by inserting his 2nd Battalion of the Guards and the grenadiers between the 23rd and 33rd Regiments. Thus regrouped, Cornwallis' men marched bravely forward to seek out the position of a probable American second line, toward which Washington and Kirkwood appeared to be retreating.

The second American line proved to be a much more difficult obstacle to overcome. The Virginia militia, strengthened on their north (right) flank by Washington's cavalry, Kirkwood's infantry, and the Virginia riflemen, maintained their positions gallantly until, at length, the superior discipline and training of the British troops started producing results. The men in the second American line began to give way, but unlike their predecessors in the first line, they did not turn and flee in one great mass. The militia north of the road began to retreat first, their lines bending back at an angle toward their comrades to the south.

The effect was like the swinging open of a huge gate. General O'Hara's grenadiers and foot guards maintained a vigorous pressure, driving their opponents before them, opening the gate wider and wider. South of the road, the hinge of the swinging gate held firm; General Leslie's men were still meeting stubborn opposition. But to the north, where the opening had first appeared, Kirkwood and Washington were again left by themselves and again fell back, this time to the third American line.

Colonel Webster, commanding the left of the advancing British, had seen the first American line disintegrate. Now the second line was giving way, and he knew it would soon dissolve under the powerful blows of O'Hara's and Leslie's troops. A huge gate had swung open before his eyes; the troops to his front had retreated. Through the trees he could discern a third American line. Without a moment's hesitation he launched the 33rd, the light infantry, and the jägers straight toward that position.

Colonel James Webster had proved on many occasions to be a capable, intelligent, brave officer, but on this occasion, he committed a grievous error. There were not enough men with him to overpower a third line which, from knowledge of Tarleton's previous experience at Cowpens, he should have known would contain General Greene's best troops. His attack should have been withheld until O'Hara and Leslie had finished their destruction of the second line. He thus denied his commander, Lord Cornwallis, an opportunity to regroup and make a coordinated effort.

Colonel Webster's assault met the fate it deserved. The Continentals waited in steady ranks until their attackers had struggled up the hill to within 100 feet and then loosed a volley of musketry upon them. Spearheaded by the 1st Maryland and Kirkwood's battered company, the Americans counterattacked and drove Webster's men at bayonet point back across a ravine and off to the side.

At this moment General Nathanael Greene held the fate of the south in the palm of his hand. Colonel Webster was hastily re-forming his soldiers. Generals O'Hara and Leslie were just completing their destruction of the second American line. The British were not in good position to withstand a determined assault. A vigorous attack might sweep them all from the field. The four regiments of Virginia and Maryland Continentals were there, waiting; if Greene gave the command they could be thrown into the battle. Cornwallis' army could be driven from the field; Cowpens might be repeated on a grander scale. With the main British army routed, the Americans could easily regain control of the Carolinas and Georgia.

Nathanael Greene was a fighting general. The temptation to hurl his Continentals against Cornwallis' army must have been very great indeed. If the other three regiments were half as good as the superb 1st Maryland, General Greene would not have hesitated for a moment. But the other three were unknown quantities, and experienced British regulars are never driven from a battlefield with ease. An attack that failed would wreck Greene's plan for defense, which was succeeding admirably. Failure would result in the loss of his army and there was no other organized force in the land to fight for the independence of the south. Any battle necessarily involves the taking of intelligent, calculated risks, but in this case, to issue the order for an attack would have been equivalent to entrusting the future of his countrymen to a gamble similar to a roll of the dice. The order was not given and no historian has ever brought to light any factors which might tend to prove that an assault would have had more than a fifty-fifty chance of success.

The preliminaries were over; the first two American lines had been dispersed; the main battle was about to begin and the odds were fairly equal because of the casualties suffered by the British during the opening stages. Now there came a short pause as Cornwallis made preparations to move against Greene's main line of resistance. The struggle that followed can most easily be described as taking place in three phases, following rapidly, one upon the heels of another: the British assault; an American counterattack stopped only by most desperate measures; another British attack and the withdrawal from the field.

While Colonel Webster engaged the attention of the Virginia Continentals at the north end of the line, Cornwallis launched his main assault. He sent the leading troops in a long, curving line through the edge of a clearing, toward the south end of the position. The full force of the British attack burst upon the untried, newly organized 5th Maryland, which broke and gave way in flight. But American reaction was instantaneous. Colonel Washington, at full gallop, crossed behind the American line to ride down upon the apparently victorious attackers. The 1st Maryland and Kirkwood's Delaware veterans hurled themselves upon the British. A terrific hand-to-hand bayonet struggle followed. Suddenly Cornwallis realized that his brave veterans, who had at last attained the third American line at such a terrible cost to themselves, were falling back. Just a few moments before, complete victory had appeared to be within their grasp, but now his stalwart soldiers were being forced to give ground under the pressure of the sudden, unexpected American counterattack. The crisis of the battle was at hand. Lord Cornwallis instantly grasped the fact that there was only one way in which he could personally intervene to save the day. Although General O'Hara, lying wounded on the ground beside the road, begged him not to do so, General Cornwallis ordered his artillery to fire point-blank into the middle of the confused, desperate melee. This drastic measure, which brought death to British and Americans alike, was undoubtedly the only means by which the 1st Maryland could have been stopped.

The next British charge, against the Virginia Continentals at the other end of the line, led by that determined officer, Colonel Webster, was again repulsed; Webster fell mortally wounded in this attack. Lord Cornwallis, aggressive as ever, was contemplating another coordinated charge but the more cautious Greene was satisfied. He withdrew his men from that bloody field.

Cornwallis claimed the victory and technically he was correct. His army of 1,900 British and Hessian regulars had driven from the field 1,820 American regulars plus 2,600 militia, but his losses had been far too heavy. His British soldiers had fought magnificently, but Greene's battle tactics, his intelligent use of the militia with the Legions, and the fighting qualities of the American soldier had cost the British Army 532 casualties, a terrible percentage, over one-fourth of the men engaged.

General Greene reported 261 killed and wounded, but the other normal categories of "captured and missing" could not be computed. Well over a thousand had disappeared from the field, but Greene was not worried by their absence, and the performance of the Virginia militia had far exceeded anyone's expectations. At this rate of exchange he could well afford to fight Cornwallis again.

In his memoirs, Lieutenant Colonel "Light Horse Harry" Lee described Cornwallis' predicament: "Nearly a third of his force slaughtered; many of his best officers killed or wounded;

and that victory for which he had so long toiled, and at length gained, bringing in its train not one solitary benefit. No body of Loyalists crowding around his standards; no friendly convoys pouring in supplies; his wants pressing; and his resources distant."

Lord Cornwallis had made a splendid effort, had almost succeeded, but not quite. Unable to stay where he was, he retreated to Wilmington, North Carolina, then decided to leave the Carolinas to the care of others and marched north toward Virginia, on a road that would eventually end at Yorktown.

10

Nathanael Greene—Washington's Best General

After the Battle of Guilford Court House, General Nathanael Greene had withdrawn from the field, but only for a very short distance. Then under a flag of truce, he sent American army surgeons back to the battlefield to help Cornwallis with the British and American sick and wounded. Two days later, General Cornwallis began to retreat, leaving a large number of his disabled men to be cared for by the Americans.

At this point it was evident to all that, although Cornwallis had apparently driven the Americans from the field of battle, the British had lost the campaign. For Cornwallis was not retreating southward the way he had come, but had turned southeast toward the port of Wilmington, and was giving back to the Americans the control of all the remainder of the State of North Carolina.

At Guilford Court House, General Greene had won back one of the three states which had fallen into British hands. Now, instead of following Cornwallis, he turned southward to try to recover the other two: South Carolina and Georgia. It was fairly obvious that Nathanael Greene's next objective would be the British garrison at Camden, but Lord Cornwallis made no attempt to provide assistance to it. By this time he had decided that Virginia might provide a more suitable territory for the exercise of his talents and hoped that the British garrisons in South Carolina and Georgia could take care of themselves. He may also have consoled himself, for his lack of effort, with the comforting thought that the distance to Camden was so great that he could not possibly arrive there ahead of Greene. And, in any event, the British garrisons in South Carolina and Georgia were powerful and could not be easily overcome. By this decision Cornwallis publicly admitted his failure to defeat General Greene and showed that he still had not fully estimated the capabilities of his erstwhile opponent. He and the other British leaders in the south were still to learn a great deal about Nathanael Greene and the latter's genius for war.

This American general from Rhode Island, who had been expelled from the Quaker Church when he entered the army, has been mentioned so often that it seems unnecessary to recall his battle experience. His ability as a leader and administrator had first attracted Washington's attention in the early days before Boston when the Rhode Island brigade presented, in contrast to all the others, an outstanding, soldierly appearance. But, like anyone else, when first learning his new profession, Greene had made mistakes. He had, for example, believed that Forts Washington and Lee could be held and had so advised Washington, almost getting himself and his command captured as a result. However, from that moment on, Nathanael Greene had been Washington's strong right arm—at Trenton, at Brandywine where his division had staved off disaster, at Germantown, and again at Monmouth Court House.

In the army's hour of need at Valley Forge, Washington had called on General Greene's remarkable organizational and administrative ability to save the army from death by starvation. The fact that any men survived the ordeal had been largely due to Greene's ability, efforts, and energy.

Now, in command of the southern department, without Washington's guidance, control, or supervision, Nathanael Greene had proved himself second to none in his ability to act as an independent commander in charge of a large theater of operations. He had more than retrieved Gates' extraordinary blunders and had completely baffled the best British general in the thirteen colonies. And, in the process, General

Greene had proved that he was not only an able tactician, but a superb strategist. Now he was about to combine both these qualities with his previously demonstrated abilities as an organizer and administrator, and also demonstrate an unusual understanding of the American soldier.

In six years of active warfare, General Greene had learned that there was no better fighter in the world than the American soldier when properly trained and well led in combat. The real problem had been to discover ways and means to utilize the services of untrained men. At Saratoga, Benedict Arnold had shown how a couple of regiments could be used in battle. Daniel Morgan had demonstrated at Cowpens that such men can be trusted to do their duty for a very short while, if they are not asked to do too much. With a few trained officers and soldiers in the ranks, militia had sometimes performed better than anyone had expected—witness Colonel Dixon's North Carolina regiment at Camden, and the Virginians in the second line at Guilford Court House.

But for a campaign designed to regain control of two entire states, Nathanael Greene knew that he would have to find some other source of strength in order to win. During his recent operations, General Greene had come to know, and appreciate, a third type of American soldier (other than the regular Continental or the militiaman), whose activities were particularly well suited to that sparsely settled, often swampy region. This third type of soldier was the partisan or guerrilla fighter who, under the leadership of such commanders as Marion, Pickens and Sumter, had been forced to acquire an unusual sort of discipline for his own preservation.

Cornwallis and most of the other senior British officers had come to look upon these guerrillas primarily as a source of extreme annoyance, who would eventually be destroyed. In due course of time the British leaders might have been correct in their analysis, but Nathanael Greene saw the partisans in a very different light and he was undoubtedly the first senior American general to do so. He fully realized that their discipline was of a different quality. They could not stand up to the British regulars in an open battle, as could his Continentals, but, in their own way, they were completely reliable and trustworthy. Furthermore, their method of operation, striking swiftly, in small bands, at isolated British outposts, was perfectly suited to the plan he had devised for recovering South Carolina and Georgia which were now occupied by a series of garrisons scattered in many places throughout the two states.

Preceding the Battle of Cowpens, General Greene had, himself, adopted their methods, by dividing his small army into two parts, neither of which could have possibly offered battle to Cornwallis' army. Now he planned a similar strategy on a grander scale. Most of his militia had gone home because their six weeks' enlistment time had expired, but the main army was still intact. Greene had with him two Maryland Continental regiments, two Virginia Continental regiments, the Delaware Continentals, and Lee's and Washington's Legions. With these units his army was formidable enough to face almost any British garrison in South Carolina, but, in addition, he could send fast-moving regular units to strengthen the hands of the partisans so that they, with his help, might be able to overpower some of the smaller British garrisons.

Greene's first move was typical of his new plan. South of Camden was a British post named Fort Watson, which was temporarily guarded by a small detachment. Lee's Legion and a few Maryland Continentals were sent to join General Francis Marion, the most capable of all the partisan leaders. Together they besieged the fort and, after erecting a wooden tower tall enough to overlook the walls of the stockade, so that marksmen from the tower could fire within the walls, rushed Fort Watson, which promptly capitulated. Thus, on April 23, 1781, fell the first of the British forts.

Simultaneously, General Greene had marched with his main body upon Camden, one of the strongest and most heavily garrisoned of the British posts in South Carolina. The com-

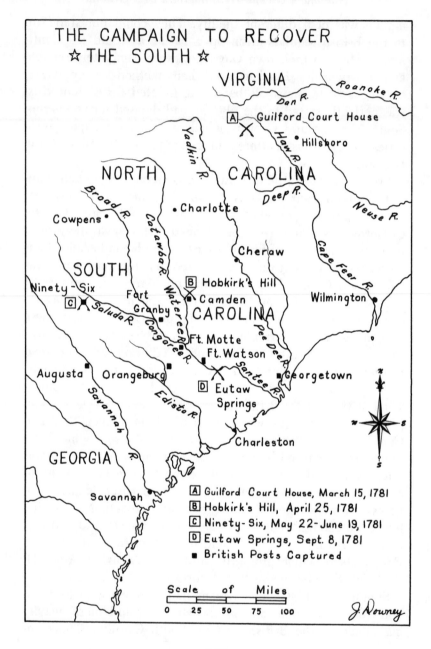

THE CAMPAIGN TO RECOVER
☆ THE SOUTH ☆

VIRGINIA

Roanoke R.

Den R.

[A] Guilford Court House

Haw R.

• Hillsboro

NORTH CAROLINA

Yadkin R.

Deep R.

Neuse R.

Broad R.

Cowpens •

Catawba R.

• Charlotte

• Cheraw

Wateree R.

Cape Fear R.

SOUTH

[B] Hobkirk's Hill

Ninety-Six

Fort Granby

[C]

Saluda R.

• Camden

CAROLINA

Wilmington •

Congaree R.

Pee Dee R.

Ft. Motte
Ft. Watson

Augusta ■ Orangeburg ■

Edisto R.

Savannah R.

Santee R.

• Georgetown

[D] Eutaw Springs

N

GEORGIA

Charleston

W E

Savannah •

S

[A] Guilford Court House, March 15, 1781
[B] Hobkirk's Hill, April 25, 1781
[C] Ninety-Six, May 22-June 19, 1781
[D] Eutaw Springs, Sept. 8, 1781
■ British Posts Captured

Scale of Miles
0   25   50   75   100

J. Downey

204

mander of this garrison was Lieutenant Colonel Lord Francis Rawdon, popularly known as "the ugliest man in the British Army," but a very able soldier who had fought with great courage as a lieutenant at Bunker Hill, and then had taken part in many of the more important battles of the war. Lord Rawdon had under his command some 900 British and Loyalist troops to face Greene's 1,300 plus 250 militia. Rawdon's position was strong. Greene would have faced a difficult obstacle if he had decided to attempt an attack, but Rawdon, upon receipt of some information about Greene's dispositions, chose to deliver an assault. The result was the Battle of Hobkirk's Hill, fought on April 25, 1781, just south of the old Camden battlefield. It was a very hotly contested struggle in which a confusing order by the regimental commander of Greene's famous 1st Maryland caused that regiment to withdraw just when victory appeared to be in sight. This led to the hasty retreat of other units, and the American army was forced to retire from the field.

General Nathanael Greene had lost his second battle, but as in the case of Guilford Court House, both armies had sustained heavy casualties. The British could not afford to stay where they were and fight another such battle with the Americans. Therefore, on May 10, two weeks after Hobkirk's Hill, Lord Rawdon, like Cornwallis after Guilford Court House, retreated, surrendering Camden to his enemy.

In the next five days events moved with astonishing rapidity. General Thomas Sumter, who at first showed no desire whatever to cooperate with Greene in any way, had failed in an independent effort to capture Fort Granby (now within the city limits of Columbia). However, on May 11, Sumter had succeeded in capturing a small British garrison at Orangeburg. On the very next day, General Francis Marion and Colonel Lee seized Fort Motte. Three days after that, on May 15, Fort Granby surrendered to "Light Horse Harry" Lee and his men. Every British post in South Carolina, with the exception of Charleston, of Ninety-Six in the western part of the state, and of Georgetown near the sea coast, had fallen to the Americans. Marion was sent to Georgetown. The garrison took one look at Marion's partisan corps, evacuated the place, and fled to Charleston. Suddenly it began to look as if the entire State of South Carolina would be recovered as easily after the British victory at Hobkirk's Hill as North Carolina had been after the British victory at Guilford Court House.

However, the fates were not going to be quite so kind to Greene and his fellow Americans in South Carolina. In the first place, Lord Rawdon was an able soldier and had no intention whatever of giving up the state without another fight, nor did the British Government. Reinforcements were already being brought by sea. General Greene, knowing nothing of these additional British troops, had already marched to besiege Ninety-Six. Enroute he had detached Lee's Legion to work with General Andrew Pickens in an attempt to secure Augusta, Georgia. Both garrisons put up a much stronger resistance than had been encountered at any of the other isolated posts and, in the meantime, the reinforcements arrived for Lord Rawdon.

The British forts at Augusta finally surrendered on June 6. Lee and Pickens promptly started for Ninety-Six to aid Greene in his siege of that valuable strongpoint, but Lord Rawdon was also marching toward the same place. The story of what occurred at Ninety-Six is worth relating in a little more detail, for here, after his whirlwind reconquest of most of the State of South Carolina, Nathanael Greene was to suffer another grievous disappointment.

The fort at Ninety-Six was commanded by Lieutenant Colonel John H. Cruger, an extremely able Loyalist from New York, and contained a garrison of 350 Loyalist troops from New York and New Jersey, plus 200 South Carolina Tory militia. Upon arrival, on May 21, the Americans found the defenses far too strong to take by assault. Therefore, General Greene immediately began regular siege operations. His engineer officer was the now-famous Thaddeus Kosciusko. Under

Kosciusko's direction, the operations were conducted vigorously, night and day. On June 8, Colonel Lee and his Legion arrived, fresh from the capture of Augusta, followed closely by General Pickens and his partisans. The Americans redoubled their efforts; success appeared imminent, although the work was interrupted continually by nightly sorties from the garrison.

Then both sides received the news that Lord Rawdon was marching with all possible speed to the relief of the garrison. Now the siege became a battle against time, with Greene determined to take the fort, and Colonel Cruger just as determined to hang on to the last man. Finally the Americans decided to launch an assault in a desperate attempt to capture the garrison before the promised relief arrived. When this attack, delivered on June 18, was repulsed after a furious struggle, with heavy losses, Greene and his army reluctantly gave up the siege and sullenly withdrew.

Lord Rawdon had saved his men from capture, but Ninety-Six was isolated, nearly 200 miles by road from Charleston. Colonel Rawdon had only three possible courses of action open to him: stay where he was; chase Greene up into North Carolina; or retreat. In spite of the fact that he had just saved the garrison, the British leader must have bitterly resented the fact that he had been forced to come to the relief of Ninety-Six at all. Over a month before, when he had decided to evacuate Camden, he had sent a message to Colonel Cruger to evacuate Ninety-Six and fall back on Augusta. That message had been intercepted by the Americans, so here he was with Ninety-Six in his possession, many dreary miles from the seacoast with no possible way to supply the fort without establishing a long line of communications stretching back to Charleston, open to attack by the Americans at any point. Furthermore, the idea of chasing Greene into North Carolina did not appeal to him at all. The outcome would most likely be a repetition of the Guilford Court House campaign. Therefore, Colonel Rawdon gave orders to evacuate Ninety-Six, demolished the fort, and withdrew to Orangeburg. General Greene followed, but, by this time, both armies were rapidly approaching a state of exhaustion. After a period of restless maneuvering, both were forced by the intense summer heat and the prevalence of malaria, which afflicted so many of the soldiers, to call a halt for rest and recuperation. Lord Rawdon, his health shattered by the rigors of the campaign, sailed for England, but misfortune continued to follow him. His ship was captured by the French Navy and he was sent to Brest as a prisoner-of-war.

The final major battle of the campaign was fought at Eutaw Springs, on September 8, 1781. In quantity and quality the troops engaged were fairly matched. The American army, commanded by General Nathanael Greene, numbered approximately 2,300 men. Of these, about 1,600 were Virginia, Maryland, Delaware, and North Carolina Continentals—infantry, artillery, and cavalry. The majority of the remainder were experienced South Carolina partisans led by General Marion and General Pickens.

The British force of about 2,000 men was commanded by Lieutenant Colonel Alexander Stuart. Although somewhat outnumbered, it was composed almost entirely of British regulars and Loyalist troops, in approximately equal numbers. The result was a particularly stubborn, hard-fought battle in which the men of both sides exhibited bravery, determination, and skill. Here, again, with triumph on a battlefield about to be his at last, Nathanael Greene saw victory torn from his grasp. The famished American soldiers, after driving their enemy from the field and seizing the British camp, suddenly halted, broke ranks, and began looting the supplies. Colonel Stuart was thus given time to reorganize, counterattack, and drive the Americans back to their starting point. The British held possession of the battlefield, but retired toward Charleston the next day. The casualties on both sides were very severe. The American total was over 520, nearly one-fourth of the number engaged, but the British and Loyalists suffered over 860, well over 40 percent of their strength.

For the fourth time in a row—Guilford Court House, Hobkirk's Hill, Ninety-Six, Eutaw Springs—General Greene had failed to achieve victory on a battlefield, but on this occasion, there was no doubt in the mind of anyone present as to whether or not the ultimate objective of the campaign had been attained. South Carolina had been recovered for the patriot cause, except for the territory around Charleston; and with Augusta captured, the State of Georgia, except for Savannah, would soon be under American control. In all the south, only these two cities, plus Wilmington in North Carolina, and Yorktown in Virginia, were still in British hands. As for the latter, General Washington was already halfway there on his march down from the Hudson Highlands.

In a campaign lasting a little less than six months, three southern states had, for all practical purposes, been regained by the Americans. Although he had not been fortunate enough to win any of the larger battles, Nathanael Greene had, by the intelligent, skillful use of both regular and irregular troops, forced his enemy to evacuate all but the major seaports. In the military history of the United States there have been very few campaigns of long duration which were as brilliantly conceived, planned, and executed. Nathanael Greene's operations to recover the south deserve to rank alongside such other masterpieces as Winfield Scott's campaign into the interior of Mexico, resulting in the capture of Mexico City; Stonewall Jackson's Valley Campaign; General Grant's operations south and east of Vicksburg, which led to the siege of that fortress; and General Douglas MacArthur's campaign to recover New Guinea, leading to the landings on the island of Leyte.

The surrender at Yorktown on October 19, 1781, is generally regarded as the signal for the end of the American Revolution. Washington's army returned to its encampments in the Hudson Highlands to watch Clinton's army in New York, and to await the coming of peace. Only a few foresaw that it would be a very long time indeed before the actual treaty would be signed, and fewer still predicted the problems that would be encountered in trying to maintain the existence of the army until the enemy publicly acknowledged defeat. With final victory in sight, the state governments lapsed into an indifference that made it extremely difficult to procure supplies for the troops. During the winter following the victory at Yorktown, and in the last winter of 1782-83, when the army was concentrated at the New Windsor Cantonment near Newburgh, New York, the soldiers again faced starvation, still unable, without pay, to provide for their nearly destitute families far away at home. For a period of nearly two years after Yorktown, their lives were as filled with hardships as during the periods when the patriot cause had seemed hopeless.

These were the difficulties that the principal army in the north had yet to endure, but Greene's little army in the south had already encountered these, and he still had a war to fight. After the Battle of Eutaw Springs he had been faced with the problem of caring for not only the American wounded, but also the British who had been left on the field, with inadequate food and medical supplies. In addition, many of those who had escaped injury during the battle were now sick with fever. In mid-September, the army was reduced to less than a thousand men fit for duty. It was the old story all over again, yet the southern army had to continue to appear to function despite its hardships.

In those days when land communications and travel were limited to the speed of a horse, or of a man on foot, the southern department had always been entirely separate. The distances between Washington and Greene were so enormous that each was forced to rely almost entirely upon his own resources. Nearly two weeks after the Yorktown surrender, and almost two months after the Battle of Eutaw Springs, reinforcements were sent to Greene. Marching at a speed of about fifteen miles a day, Major General Arthur St. Clair and Brigadier General Anthony Wayne made the long trek toward

Charleston with 2,000 Continentals. It took them just over two months to complete their wearisome march. But news of their coming had preceded them and had caused the British commander at Wilmington to evacuate that city. Upon their arrival, Greene sent Wayne down into Georgia with a small force. It took exactly six months for Wayne's men, aided by Georgia and South Carolina volunteers, to clear the state of its Tory partisans and cause the evacuation of Savannah, July 11, 1782. This left only Charleston. Operations continued there for another five months before the garrison finally sailed away on December 14, 1782.

Upon the conclusion of his operations General Nathanael Greene was handsomely rewarded by both South Carolina and North Carolina. The State of Georgia presented him with a beautiful plantation near Savannah. When he rode northward to rejoin Washington at New Windsor, he found that he had become a hero in the north as well as in the south.

It is a generally accepted truth that, at the beginning, no one other than George Washington could have held the thirteen colonies together through the dark and trying years of the American Revolution. However, if near the end, something had happened to Washington and it had been necessary to appoint another commander-in-chief, there would have been only one logical choice. The man chosen would have surely been Washington's own choice to command the southern department, Nathanael Greene.

Throughout the war only one man, other than Washington, had consistently proved himself competent as a battlefield leader, and also as an organizer and administrator on a large scale. Several generals had demonstrated their ability to command portions of armies in combat. A few had shown that they were capable of exercising independent command of large units in battle. Of all Washington's generals, only five had ever been given the responsibility of commanding a separate department.

Early in the war General Charles Lee had been appointed

to the command of the southern department. He had been present in Charleston when the British had made their unsuccessful attack against the city late in June, 1776. His career had ended in complete disaster at the Battle of Monmouth.

The next commander of the southern department had been General Benjamin Lincoln. His tenure of office had lasted about eighteen months, until May, 1780, when he had been forced to surrender his entire army at Charleston.

Lincoln's successor had been General Horatio Gates who had shown administrative ability as Washington's adjutant general during the early part of the war at the Siege of Boston, and had become famous because Burgoyne's army had surrendered to him at Saratoga. General Gates' incapacity had been thoroughly demonstrated on the battlefield of Camden on August 16, 1780.

This left only two out of five, and both of these two, Philip Schuyler and Nathanael Greene, had demonstrated that they were thoroughly capable of organizing and administering a separate department under the worst possible conditions. Because of the political intrigues against him, General Schuyler was never given a chance to lead troops in combat. For various reasons, however, it is doubtful that he would have been as successful as General Greene. The record indicates that Schuyler lacked some of the qualities needed to inspire his men to endure continued hardship, misery, and privation. The officers and men of his own State of New York followed him willingly; soldiers from other states accepted his leadership; but those from New England distrusted him violently.

It is rather remarkable how readily General Greene was accepted by the officers and soldiers of the southern states because, after all was said and done, he was a New Englander. Perhaps in those days when men's memories of the beginnings of the individual colonies were fresher, the southerners took into account the fact that he came from Rhode Island which had been founded by people fleeing from persecution in Puritan Massachusetts. Certainly, however, when General Greene arrived to take command, the people of the south were well acquainted with his reputation as a battlefield leader, in command of both northern and southern troops on numerous occasions in Pennsylvania, New York, and New Jersey, and remembered with gratitude his fair and impartial treatment of all who suffered the horrors of Valley Forge.

In any list of Americans who fought and won the War for Independence, the name Nathanael Greene should stand next to the name George Washington. Yet, in the strange way that history sometimes becomes distorted, although the Father of our Country will always be remembered with pride, the fame of his best general has suffered a gradual decline. The names of many other lesser men, whose contributions toward the winning of the war were small by comparison, are much better known today.

It is most unfortunate that General Nathanael Greene's name does not always appear in the top rank of the heroes of this nation in the north, but it is particularly unfortunate in the south, where military virtues are generally more highly regarded than elsewhere. He is one New England Yankee who should be remembered with pride and affection by all sections of this country.

Bibliography

The books listed below are those that proved most helpful in the preparation of this volume. A longer bibliography would present a more comprehensive picture of the number of books consulted. However, such a list, including books primarily devoted to different leaders or battles, naval warfare, or other aspects of the Revolution, would not be as accurate a guide to the sources utilized.

Alden, John R., *The American Revolution, 1775-1783.* New York, Harper and Brothers, 1954.

Anderson, Troyer S., *The Command of the Howe Brothers during the American Revolution.* New York & London, Oxford University Press, 1936.

Bilias, George A. (ed.) *George Washington's Generals.* New York, William Morrow & Company, 1964.

Bill, Alfred H., *Valley Forge, The Making of an Army.* New York, Harper and Brothers, 1952.

Bird, Harrison, *March to Saratoga.* New York, Oxford University Press, 1963.

Bridenbaugh, Carl, *Cities in Revolt.* New York, Alfred A. Knopf, Inc., 1955.

Callahan, North, *Henry Knox, George Washington's General.* New York, Rinehart & Company, Inc., 1958.

——*Daniel Morgan, Ranger of the Revolution.* New York, Holt, Rinehart & Winston, 1961.

Carrington, Gen. Henry B., *Battles of the American Revolution.* New York, A. S. Barnes & Company, 1888.

Clinton, Lt. Gen. Sir Henry, *The American Rebellion,* abridgement of the *Clinton Papers,* edited by William B. Willcox. New York, Yale University Press, 1954.

Commager, Henry S., and Morris, Richard B. (eds.), *The Spirit of Seventy-Six.* Indianapolis & New York, The Bobbs-Merrill Company, Inc., 1958.

De Fonblanque, Edward B., *Political and Military Episodes . . . Life and Correspondence of the Right Hon. John Burgoyne.* London, Macmillan & Co., Ltd., 1876.

Dictionary of American Biography, edited by Allen Johnson. New York, Charles Scribner's Sons.

Dupuy, Col. R. Ernest, and Dupuy, Col. Trevor N., *The Compact History of the Revolutionary War.* New York, Hawthorn Books, Inc., 1963.

Esposito, Col. Vincent J. (ed.), *The West Point Atlas of American Wars.* New York, Frederick A. Praeger, Inc., 1959.

Fisher, Sydney G., *The Struggle for American Independence.* Philadelphia & London, J. B. Lippincott Company, 1908.

Fiske, John, *The American Revolution.* Boston & New York, Houghton Mifflin Company, 1896.

Fitzpatrick, John C. (ed.), *The Writings of George Washington.* Washington, D. C., U. S. Government Printing Office, 1931-44.

Fortescue, Sir John W., *History of the British Army.* London, The Macmillan Company, 1899-1930.

Freeman, Douglas S., *George Washington, A Biography,* Vols. IV & V. New York, Charles Scribner's Sons, 1951-52.

Frothingham, Capt. Thomas G., *Washington, Commander in Chief.* Boston & New York, Houghton Mifflin Company, 1930.

Ganoe, Col. William A., *The History of the United States Army.* New York, D. Appleton-Century Company, Inc., 1942.

Greene, Francis V., *General Greene.* New York, D. Appleton & Company, 1893.

Greene, George W., *The Life of Nathanael Greene, Major-General in the Army of the Revolution.* Vol. I: New York, G. P. Putnam's Sons, 1867; Vols. II & III: New York, Hurd & Houghton, 1871.

Headley, Joel T., *Washington and His Generals.* New York, Baker & Scribner, 1848.

Higginbotham, Don, *Daniel Morgan, Revolutionary Rifleman.* Chapel Hill, North Carolina, The University of North Carolina Press, 1961.

Hudleston, F. J., *Gentleman Johnny Burgoyne.* Garden City, New York, Garden City Publishing Co., Inc., 1927.

Johnston, Henry P., *The Storming of Stony Point.* New York, James T. White & Company, 1900.

Lancaster, Bruce, *From Lexington to Liberty.* Garden City, New York, Doubleday & Company, Inc., 1955.

Lee, Maj. Gen. Henry, *Memoirs of the War in the Southern Department of the United States.* New York, University Publishing Company, 1869.

Lossing, Benson J., *The Pictorial Field-book of the Revolution.* New York, Harper and Brothers, 1855.

MacMunn, Lt. Gen. Sir George F., *The American War of Independence in Perspective.* London, George Bell & Sons, Ltd., 1939.

Miller, John C., *Triumph of Freedom, 1775-1783.* Boston, Little, Brown & Company, 1948.

Bibliography

Mitchell, Lt. Col. Joseph B., *Decisive Battles of the American Revolution.* New York, G. P. Putnam's Sons, 1962.

—— and Creasy, Sir Edward S., *Twenty Decisive Battles of the World.* New York, The Macmillan Company, 1964.

Mitchell, Col. William A., *Outlines of the World's Military History.* Washington, D. C., The Infantry Journal, 1931.

Montross, Lynn, *Rag, Tag and Bobtail.* New York, Harper and Brothers, 1952.

Nickerson, Hoffman, *The Turning Point of the Revolution.* Boston & New York, Houghton Mifflin Company, 1928.

Partridge, Bellamy, *Sir Billy Howe.* London, New York, and Toronto, Longmans, Green & Company, 1932.

Peckham, Howard H., *The War for Independence.* Chicago, The University of Chicago Press, 1958.

Rankin, Hugh F., *The American Revolution.* New York, G..P. Putnam's Sons, 1964.

Reed, John F., *Campaign to Valley Forge.* Philadelphia, University of Pennsylvania Press, 1965.

Roberts, Kenneth, *The Battle of Cowpens.* Garden City, New York, Doubleday & Company, Inc., 1958.

Scheer, George F., and Rankin, Hugh F., *Rebels and Redcoats.* Cleveland & New York, The World Publishing Company, 1957.

Spears, John R., *Anthony Wayne.* New York, D. Appleton & Company, 1903.

Stedman, Charles, *The History . . . of the American War.* Dublin, Printed for Messrs. P. Wogan, P. Byrne, J. Moore & W. Jones, 1794.

Steele, Maj. Matthew F., *American Campaigns.* Washington, D. C., Byron S. Adams, 1909.

Stillé, Charles J., *Major-General Anthony Wayne.* Philadelphia, J. B. Lippincott Company, 1893.

Thayer, Theodore, *Nathanael Greene, Strategist of the American Revolution.* New York, Twayne Publishers, Inc., 1960.

Trevelyan, Sir George O., *The American Revolution.* New York & London, Longmans, Green & Company, 1907-08.

—— *George the Third and Charles Fox.* New York & London, Longmans, Green & Company, 1921-27.

Upton, Maj. Gen. Emory, *The Military Policy of the United States.* Washington, D. C., U. S. Government Printing Office, 1911.

Wallace, Willard M., *Appeal to Arms.* New York, Harper and Brothers, 1951.

—— *Traitorous Hero, the Life and Fortunes of Benedict Arnold.* New York, Harper and Brothers, 1954.

Ward, Christopher, *The War of the Revolution.* New York, The Macmillan Company, 1952.

Wilkin, Capt. Walter H., *Some British Soldiers in America.* London, Hugh Rees, Ltd., 1914.

Willcox, William B., *Portrait of a General, Sir Henry Clinton in the War of Independence.* New York, Alfred A. Knopf, Inc., 1964.

Wrong, George M., *Washington and His Comrades in Arms.* New Haven, Yale University Press, 1921.

Index

219

Index

220

Index

Index

Index